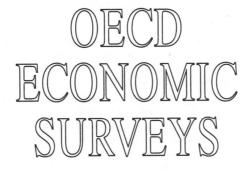

OECD ECONOMIC SURVEYS

1993-1994

UNITED KINGDOM

ORGANISATION FOR ECONOMIC CO-OPERATION AND DEVELOPMENT

ORGANISATION FOR ECONOMIC CO-OPERATION AND DEVELOPMENT

Pursuant to Article 1 of the Convention signed in Paris on 14th December 1960, and which came into force on 30th September 1961, the Organisation for Economic Co-operation and Development (OECD) shall promote policies designed:

- to achieve the highest sustainable economic growth and employment and a rising standard of living in Member countries, while maintaining financial stability, and thus to contribute to the development of the world economy;
- to contribute to sound economic expansion in Member as well as non-member countries in the process of economic development; and
- to contribute to the expansion of world trade on a multilateral, non-discriminatory basis in accordance with international obligations.

The original Member countries of the OECD are Austria, Belgium, Canada, Denmark, France, Germany, Greece, Iceland, Ireland, Italy, Luxembourg, the Netherlands, Norway, Portugal, Spain, Sweden, Switzerland, Turkey, the United Kingdom and the United States. The following countries became Members subsequently through accession at the dates indicated hereafter: Japan (28th April 1964), Finland (28th January 1969), Australia (7th June 1971), New Zealand (29th May 1973) and Mexico (18th May 1994). The Commission of the European Communities takes part in the work of the OECD (Article 13 of the OECD Convention).

3 2280 00497 9720

Publié également en français.

Table of contents

Boxes

Tables

Text

Diagrams

Text

BASIC STATISTICS OF THE UNITED KINGDOM

THE LAND

Area (1 000 sq. km)	241	Major cities (population in millions,	
Agricultural area (1 000 sq. km), 1992	185	1992 mid-year estimates):	
		Greater London	6.9
		Birmingham	1.0
		Glasgow	0.7
		Leeds	0.7
		Sheffield	0.5

THE PEOPLE

Population (30.6.1992), thousands	57 998	Total civilian employment, thousands,	
Number of inhabitants per sq. km	241	June 1993	24 658
Net increase in population, 1982-92,		*of which:*	
annual average, thousands	153	Agriculture	549
Percentage change at annual rate, 1982-92	0.3	Industry (incl. construction)	6 342
		Other activities	17 767

THE GOVERNMENT

Public sector current expenditure on goods		Composition of House of Commons, April 1992	
and services, 1993 (per cent of GDP)	22	(number of seats):	
Public sector current receipts, 1993		Conservative	336
(per cent of GDP)	36	Labour	271
Net public debt, 31st March 1993		Liberal	20
(ratio to GDP)	33	Plaid Cymru	4
		Scottish National Party	3
		Other	17
			651

FOREIGN TRADE

Exports of goods and services as a percentage		Imports of goods and services as a percentage	
of GDP, 1993	25	of GDP, 1993	27
Main exports (percentage of total exports		Main imports (percentage of total imports	
in 1993):		in 1993):	
Food, beverages and tobacco	7	Food, beverages and tobacco	10
Basic materials	2	Basic materials	4
Fuels	7	Fuels	5
Semi-manufactured goods	29	Semi-manufactured goods	26
Manufactured goods	53	Manufactured goods	54
Other	2	Other	1

THE CURRENCY

Monetary unit: Pound sterling	Currency unit per US$, average of daily figures:	
	Year 1993	0.6660
	April 1994	0.6741

Note: An international comparison of certain basic statistics is given in an annex table.

This Survey is based on the Secretariat's study prepared for the annual review of the United Kingdom by the Economic and Development Review Committee on 5th May 1994.

•

After revisions in the light of discussions during the review, final approval of the Survey for publication was given by the Committee on 30th May 1994.

•

The previous Survey of the United Kingdom was issued in January 1993.

Introduction

By early 1994, the United Kingdom had recorded eight quarters of moderate output growth in the aftermath of its longest post-war recession, returning the level of output to its mid-1990 peak. Employment started to rise in the second-half of 1993, having fallen by 1.9 million peak to trough. Continuing economic slack, low pay increases and good productivity performance have combined to reduce inflation to levels unseen in a generation. The strength of disinflation was remarkable, more than offsetting the effects of the surge in import prices following sterling's suspension from the Exchange Rate Mechanism in September 1992. Continuing modest economic recovery and low inflation are expected over the coming two years.

Chapter I discusses salient features of the current economic recovery, focusing on the adjustment of household and business sector balance-sheet positions following the rapid build-up of private debt in the late 1980s and the subsequent slump in asset prices. Labour market and wage/price developments are then reviewed. This is followed by a survey of balance of payments developments after the drop in sterling's effective rate.

Macroeconomic policies are discussed in Chapter II. The priorities of macroeconomic policy are to restore sound public sector finances and to lock in low inflation over the medium-term. Public sector borrowing has been heavily influenced by the legacy of recession, and measures were taken in the March and November 1993 budgets to rebalance fiscal policy. As in other OECD countries, ageing populations will increase spending pressure in the years ahead, although existing social programmes are generally designed to cope better with such pressure. These issues are also taken up in Chapter IV. Monetary policy is reviewed in the context of the government's new monetary policy framework. Economic prospects over the coming two years are then assessed in a final section of this chapter.

As in other OECD countries, health care accounts for one of the largest government expenditure items and often faces upward pressures. The United Kingdom now spends some 6 per cent of GDP on the National Health Service (NHS), which is significantly less than in other large OECD countries for comparable health outcomes. To improve efficiency and the quality of health care, the government introduced radical reforms in the NHS in 1991. These are discussed in Chapter III; a preliminary assessment of the reforms is presented as well as areas warranting further attention. Recent initiatives in structural reform more generally are outlined in Chapter IV. Conclusions to the Survey are given in Chapter V.

I.   Economic developments

Overview

The pace of economic recovery strengthened in the last half of 1993, and by the first quarter of 1994 total output was 2.6 per cent higher than a year earlier (Diagram 1). Low interest rates eased the burden of debt service on balance sheets, and household saving ratios fell further during 1993. The non-financial corporate sector (NFCS) moved into financial surplus after five years of deficits. Modest employment growth resumed in the second half of 1993 and unemployment in March 1994 was 250 thousand lower than at the end of 1992. Towards the end of 1993, wage settlements and average earnings growth had dropped to 25-30 year lows of some 2 and 3 per cent, respectively, though earnings growth has, not surprisingly, picked up a little in early 1994. Weak world commodity and oil prices, strong competition and good productivity gains broadly stabilised total unit costs, and increases in the retail prices index-excluding mortgage payments (RPIX) fell through the year. In March 1994, the rise in RPIX reached its lowest level since 1967, confounding the predictions of many analysts following the drop in sterling's effective rate in late 1992.

Recent economic developments

The growth in retail sales strengthened in the three months to March 1994, while manufacturing output recovered following stagnation in the fourth quarter. New car sales and housing starts remained strong. Unemployment continued to decline, falling to 9.7 per cent of the labour force in March, 0.8 percentage points lower than its December 1992 peak. Output growth is estimated to have remained close to an annual rate of 3 per cent in early 1994. Producer and retail price

Diagram 1. **KEY ASPECTS OF ECONOMIC ACTIVITY**

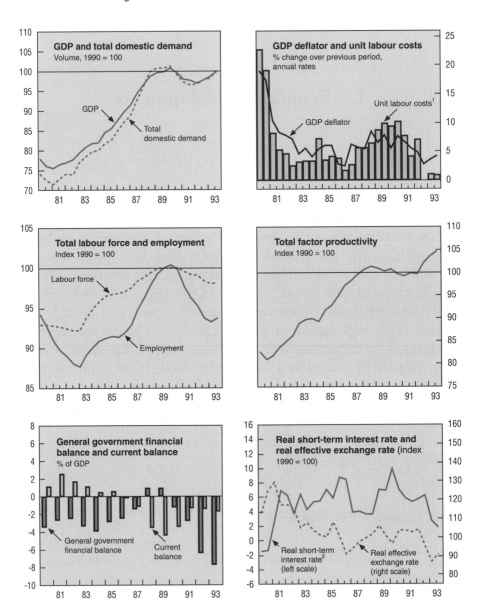

1. Total economy.
2. Three-month interbank rate adjusted by the GDP deflator.
Source: OECD, *National Accounts, Main Economic Indicators.*

increases remained subdued in an environment of weak import prices and negative producer input price inflation.

Restoring private sector finances

The current economic recovery has been dominated by on-going efforts of households and firms to adjust balance sheet positions (with consequences for public sector finances). Private sector adjustment has reached an advanced stage, but when it will be completed is difficult to judge. Private and total debt rose

Table 1. **Demand and output**

Percentage volume changes, 1990 prices

	1987	1988	1989	1990	1991	1992	1993	1993[1]			
								Q1	Q2	Q3	Q4
Private consumption	5.3	7.5	3.2	0.6	−2.2	0.0	2.5	2.0	2.1	2.7	3.2
Government consumption	1.0	0.7	1.4	2.5	2.5	0.7	−0.5	−1.1	−1.3	0.8	−0.3
Gross fixed investment	10.2	13.5	5.5	−3.4	−9.8	−1.6	0.8	0.8	−0.1	1.0	1.4
of which:											
Public[2]	−9.9	−11.0	24.0	12.0	−5.9	9.8	1.6	20.5	4.4	0.4	−17.8
Private residential	7.6	18.6	−7.6	−16.0	−15.7	5.2	−1.0	−4.1	5.2	−0.4	−4.3
Private non-residential	17.3	17.8	6.2	−3.3	−9.5	−5.9	1.0	−3.9	−2.5	1.5	9.0
Final domestic demand	5.2	7.2	3.3	0.2	−2.7	−0.2	1.6	1.1	1.0	2.0	2.1
Stockbuilding[3]	0.1	0.7	−0.3	−0.9	−0.7	0.5	0.4	0.4	0.6	−0.5	1.2
Total domestic demand	5.3	7.9	2.9	−0.6	−3.3	0.4	2.0	1.5	1.6	1.5	3.3
Exports	5.8	0.5	4.7	5.1	−0.9	3.0	3.1	4.5	2.1	5.0	1.0
Imports	7.8	12.6	7.4	0.5	−5.4	6.3	3.5	5.0	1.3	2.9	4.7
Foreign balance[3]	−0.5	−2.9	−0.8	1.1	1.2	−0.9	−0.2	−0.2	−0.2	0.5	−1.1
Statistical discrepancy[3]	0.0	0.0	0.0	0.0	−0.1	−0.1	0.0	0.0	0.0	0.1	0.1
GDP at market prices	4.8	5.0	2.2	0.4	−2.2	−0.6	1.9	1.3	1.8	2.1	2.4
Memorandum items:											
Output measure of GDP	4.6	5.0	2.2	0.6	−2.3	−0.5	1.9	1.4	1.7	2.2	2.5
Manufacturing production	4.6	7.0	4.5	−0.2	−5.3	−0.8	1.7	1.9	2.0	1.6	2.2
Employment[4]	2.4	3.4	2.7	0.3	−3.1	−2.5	−1.1	−2.4	−1.7	−0.1	0.1
Unemployment rate[4]	9.8	7.8	6.1	5.9	8.2	9.9	10.2	10.4	10.4	10.3	9.9
Real personal disposable											
income	3.4	6.0	4.9	2.1	−0.5	2.5	1.5	3.2	1.6	0.7	0.6
Personal saving ratio	7.1	5.7	7.2	8.6	10.1	12.3	11.5	12.6	12.2	11.0	10.2

1. From same period a year earlier.
2. General government and public corporations. Figures are affected by the privatisation programme.
3. Changes as a percentage of GDP from the same period a year earlier.
4. Yearly figures are averages of quarterly data for the months of March, June, September and December.
Source: Central Statistical Office, *Economic Trends,* and Department of Employment.

Diagram 2. **THE CURRENT EXPANSION COMPARED**

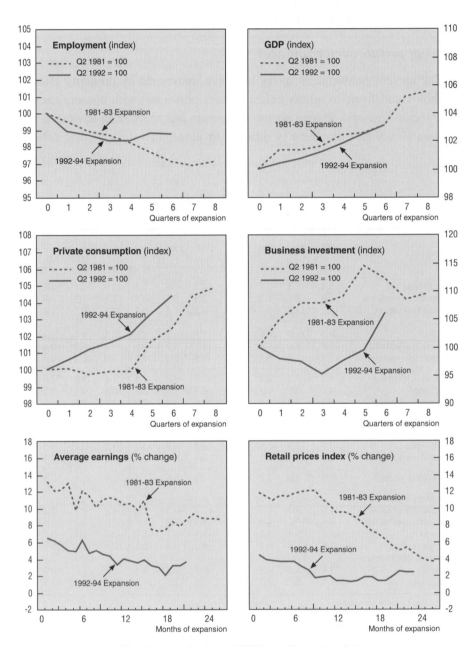

Source: Central Statistical Office, *Economic Trends*; and OECD, *Main Economic Indicators.*

Diagram 3. **CONTRIBUTIONS TO GDP GROWTH**

As a percentage change of GDP in previous year

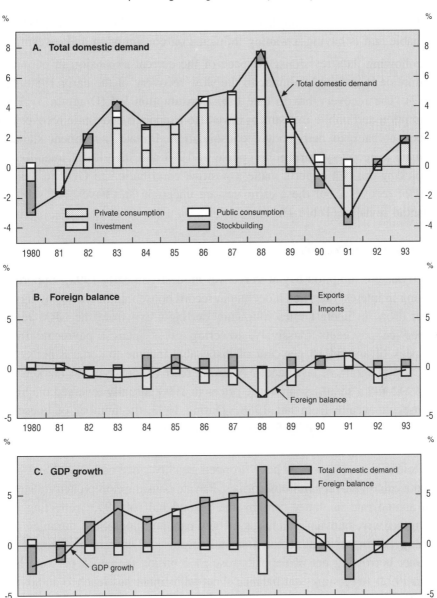

Source: Central Statistical Office.

15

more rapidly between 1989 and 1992 than between 1929 and 1932, but the absolute fall in the price level in the earlier period led to a much sharper increase in real debt burdens.[1] This burden also rose in the 1990s, but it now appears to be sustainable and is having a waning influence on consumption and investment.

Following data revisions, the pace of the current expansion in output and consumption is strikingly similar to the slow recovery of the early 1980s (Diagram 2). The recovery has to date been consumption led (Diagram 3). Public consumption and public investment have also supported economic recovery, but will be cut back to help budget consolidation. Private investment started to contribute to recovery during the course of 1993 and investment intentions are now picking-up. Net exports made a positive contribution to GDP in the early phases of recovery, but these estimates are uncertain and have been subject to substantial revision (Table 1).

A consumer-led recovery

Private consumption began to recover modestly in early 1992, supported by an easing in interest rates and a decline in record household financial savings. Yet sharper drops in interest rates following sterling's exit from the ERM reduced debt-service payments massively, lowering gross interest payments from a 1990 peak of around 15 per cent of disposable income to some 8 per cent by mid-1993 (Diagram 4, last panel). A strong recovery in financial markets from early 1992 and a small rise in house prices in 1993 partially reversed the big fall in household wealth from late 1988.[2] During 1993, the number of households with negative housing equity fell by almost one third, from a peak of 1.8 million to 1.3 million.[3]

Household savings rates have dropped steadily since early 1992 and before any noticeable recovery in house prices. Private consumption picked up strongly to an annual rate of 4 per cent by the second half of 1993, reflecting rising housing activity, buoyant purchases of new cars and household durables, and a matching fall in personal sector financial surpluses (Diagram 5). During 1993, consumer borrowing net of deposits rose £1.5 billion (some 25 per cent higher than in 1992) suggesting that balance sheet adjustment has reached an advanced stage. This is key to continuing economic recovery, as households face markedly higher tax burdens and weak disposable income growth over the coming two years.

Diagram 4. **PERSONAL SECTOR DEVELOPMENTS**

Per cent of disposable income

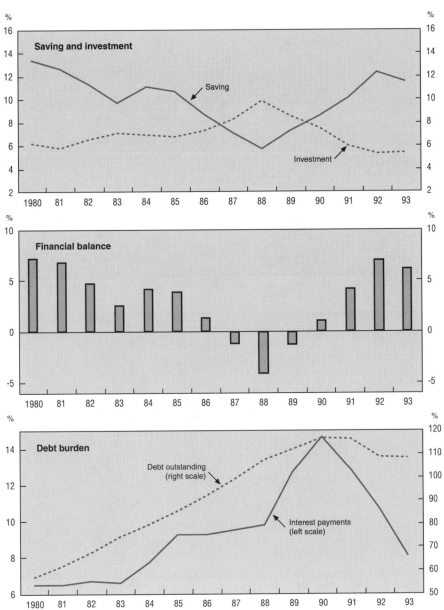

Source: Central Statistical Office, *Financial Statistics.*

17

Diagram 5. **FACTORS AFFECTING CONSUMPTION**

Index 1990 = 100

Index 1990 = 100

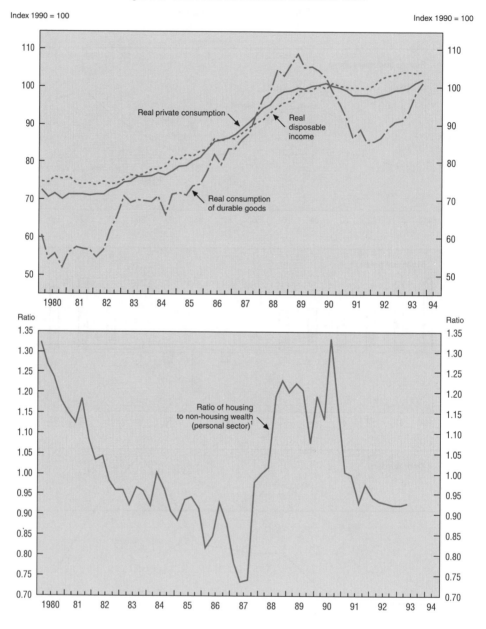

Real private consumption

Real disposable income

Real consumption of durable goods

Ratio of housing to non-housing wealth (personal sector)[1]

1. OECD estimates as from Q2 1992.
Source: Central Statistical Office, *Economic Trends;* Bank of England.

The reaction of consumers to tax increases in April 1994 is unclear, but judging by key financial ratios, balance sheet positions are such that they are capable of absorbing these increases through lower savings. Consumption growth could slow, though there was no indication of any anticipatory slowdown in retail sales in early 1994. Debt to income levels remain historically high (albeit partly reflecting one-time portfolio shifts following financial market liberalisation) (*cf.* Diagram 4, lower panel). Large numbers of households with negative housing equity and mortgage arrears will continue to weigh on house prices and restrain the household sector from increasing its net debt.

Assessing the strength of consumption is difficult, as perceptions of "steady-state" debt and wealth to income ratios have shifted radically since financial liberalisation in the late 1980s. Despite lower debt-service, the real burden of debt is high, as inflation and asset price outcomes have been lower than many debtors had anticipated. Another difficulty in assessing consumer behaviour is the high degree of instability in UK savings compared with other G-7 countries. This reflects *inter alia* the dominance of variable rate mortgages and the very high degree of leveraging in the United Kingdom.[4] Such institutional arrangements magnify the effects of nominal shocks, raising hard-to-predict precautionary savings.

From late 1988 to early 1990, real short-term interest rates rose from around 3.5 to 10 per cent (*cf.* Diagram 1), resulting in a big shift in income distribution. Households' debt-service rose from some 8 to 15 per cent of personal income, creating severe budget constraints, especially for households with large mortgages.[5] This jump in debt-service has now been reversed, but a repetition of the boom-bust cycle could eventually re-emerge. Institutional and behavioural changes to encourage lenders and borrowers to make greater use of fixed-rate contracts in a low inflation environment could reduce this risk.[6]

Investment and stockbuilding

Companies have been slow to invest so far in this recovery, partly because the debts they took on in the late 1980s and the legacy of recession put a severe squeeze on the NFCS' financial positions[7] (Diagram 6). Although business

Diagram 6. **CORPORATE SECTOR FINANCING**

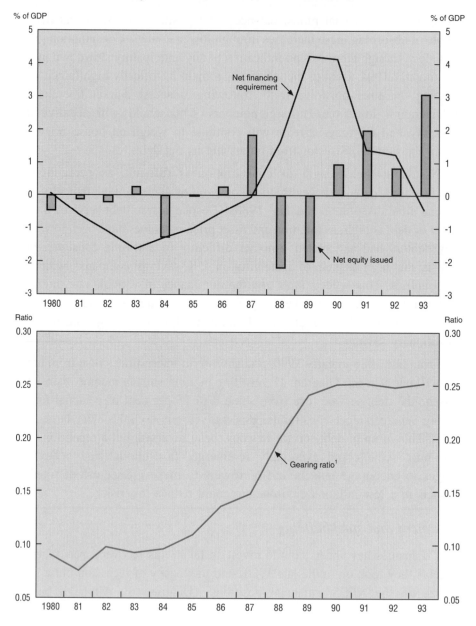

1. Ratio of business debt to business capital stock at replacement cost.
Source: Central Statistical Office, *Financial Statistics.*

investment was cut back sharply, as a proportion of GDP, it has been more resilient during this economic cycle (8 per cent of GDP in 1992 compared with 6.5 per cent in 1981). This has reflected higher profitability and on-going investment projects by the newly privatised firms and the energy sector. Public investment in transport and social infrastructure was a major source of strength in 1992 and 1993, but will be scaled back in the coming years.

Over the past 20 years, the NFCS has tended to record a balanced financial position or a small surplus to finance overseas or financial investment, where rates of return are high compared with domestic physical capital. The record financial deficits of over 4 per cent of GDP in 1989 and 1990 were unusual, initially reflecting the lagged effects of booming business investment and high dividend pay-outs on cash flow. The NFCS faced problems of indebtedness and massive financial deficits eventually triggered a record number of bankruptcies, provoking rapid cut-backs in manning levels, stocks and investment – thereby exacerbating the effects of the slump in private consumption (cf. Diagram 6, lower panel).

With households running large financial surpluses, the NFCS was unable to restore financial balance until mid-1993, on the back of a pick-up in activity, higher capacity utilisation, lower debt service, on-going cost cutting and a big rise in retained earnings. Against this background, the NFCS continued to restructure their balance sheets in 1993 rather than invest. Bank debt has been reduced and there has been a large switch to capital market financing.[8]

The process of corporate balance sheet adjustment has now reached a relatively mature stage, and the slowing foreseen in private and public consumption could be partly offset by a cyclical recovery in investment and stockbuilding. The degree of under-utilised capacity has fallen over the past two years and business confidence has strengthened. Recent CBI Surveys indicate that under 60 per cent of manufacturing firms are working below capacity (the lowest figure since 1990) and that 25 per cent of firms plan to invest to expand capacity (the highest since mid-1990). The early-1994 rise in long-term interest rates could damp the recovery in business investment, but business is much less dependent on long-term debt finance than in most other countries and the outlook for corporate cash-flow is good.

Inventories should also support output growth in the coming years, albeit to a much smaller extent than in past economic recoveries. Manufacturers' stocks fell in 15 out of 17 quarters to the fourth quarter of 1993, though distributors' stocks fell in only 10 of these quarters. This is a somewhat longer drop than in the early 1980s recession, and falling stocks a year and a half into recovery are unusual. Improvements in inventory control (*e.g.* just-in time production techniques) and pressures to cut costs have outweighed the cyclical effects of higher work-in-progress, although voluntary stockbuilding re-emerged in the last quarter of 1993.

Output patterns

The early phases of recovery have been led by consumption (and exports). Since early 1992, output in goods producing industries has recovered broadly in line with overall GDP, but the level of output is still below its 1990 peak. By early 1994, consumer goods output was up almost 5 per cent from its 1991 trough, but still 1¾ per cent below its peak. Investment goods output was about 3¾ per cent above its early 1992 trough, though it still showed a shortfall from its peak of almost 7½ per cent. In the hard hit construction sector, output stabilised in 1993, but was still 15 per cent below peak levels. By contrast, output in service industries had mostly surpassed earlier peaks by mid-1993.

Such diverse sectoral output trends make it difficult to judge the size of the "output gap". Mid-cycle trends and production function estimates (based on trend productivity and labour supply) continue to give quite large output gaps.[9] Some analysts argue that these are severely overstated because hysteresis of both labour and capital have made effective gaps quite small. These factors are relevant, but frequently overstated. Long-term unemployment has risen less than in the 1980s and capital obsolescence is less severe, because manufacturing is now a smaller part of the economy and the recession also touched the less capital intensive service sectors. More fundamentally, potential output is not an exogenous constraint, but can be affected by supply-side policies and by higher demand. Indeed, in the past, higher demand has also engendered more effective supply. And the strong degree of disinflation (see below) is difficult to explain in the absence of substantial output gaps and/or greater supply-side flexibility (see below).

22

Labour market developments

A striking feature of the recovery was the early drop in unemployment starting in January 1993, bringing registered unemployment down 250 thousand by March 1994. In the early 1970s, unemployment fell only from the third year of recovery; in the 1980s, it took five years of recovery before unemployment fell. In contrast to most EU countries, UK unemployment peaked at a lower level this time than in the previous cycle in the 1980s, although at that time the population of working age was increasing much more rapidly than of late. To some extent, this can be attributed to labour market deregulation and changes in the tax and transfer system introduced in the 1980s[10] which have promoted modest real wage outcomes and more flexible employment practices.

When unemployment initially dropped in early 1993, many analysts attributed this to a one-time employment level adjustment, following the perhaps excessive labour market correction in the wake of the sharp fall in business confidence after sterling's suspension from the ERM. In the event, the modest pick-up in employment through 1993 indicates that underlying labour market conditions are firming slowly, albeit from a patchy base and that hiring and firing decisions have quickened (*cf.* Diagram 2). Job vacancies have risen since late 1991, but average hours worked have fallen and numbers on short-time work in manufacturing increased. Labour supply conditions have also aided the fall in unemployment – with fewer 16-24 year olds entering the labour force and larger numbers staying on into higher education (Table 2).

In the third quarter of 1993, employment (employer based) started to increase, rising by 111 000. But, job creation was more than accounted for by continued growth in part-time employment. Full-time employment fell marginally (reflecting a fall in the male component). In the fourth quarter, total employment was broadly unchanged, and there was no further shift towards part-time employment, though male employment fell a little, matched by a small rise in female employment. To some extent, this pattern reflected continuing downsizing and cost-cutting in manufacturing and construction, where full-time male jobs dominate, and is one reason why long-term unemployment has hit adult males hard (Diagram 7). By contrast, steady service sector output growth facilitated part-time work, notably in the retailing and hotel and catering sectors.[11] Workplace surveys show that seven out of eight of those working part-time do so by choice. While part-time and full-time workers are not perfect substitutes,

Table 2. **The labour market**

	1988	1989	1990	1991	1992	1993	1993 Q2	1993 Q3	1993 Q4	1994 Q1
	Percentage changes from previous period, seasonally adjusted annual rates									
Working population[1]	1.2	0.9	0.1	-0.6	-0.7	-0.7	-0.3	1.4	-1.9	..
Employment total	3.4	2.7	0.4	-3.1	-2.5	-1.1	0.0	1.8	-0.1	..
Employees	3.0	1.8	0.5	-2.8	-2.1	-1.0	-0.1	1.6	-0.9	..
of which:										
Manufacturing	1.2	0.2	-2.1	-6.6	-4.9	-2.5	-0.5	0.9	-0.5	..
Government	0.5	-2.7	0.4	-2.7	-4.2	..	..	..		
Self employed	5.9	7.1	0.7	-4.2	-4.4	-0.9	6.6	4.4	4.1	..
Employed ratio (level)	70.1	72.0	72.2	69.6	67.8	66.8	66.7	67.0	67.0	..
	Monthly averages (levels)									
Unfilled vacancies[2] (1 000)	248.6	219.5	173.6	117.9	117.1	127.9	123.4	128.1	138.9	140.6
Numbers unemployed-claimant count										
Adjusted (1 000)	2 272.8	1 782.2	1 660.8	2 286.1	2 765.0	2 900.6	2 925.6	2 913.6	2 811.5	2 755.4
Unemployment rate-claimant count										
Adjusted[3]	8.1	6.3	5.8	8.1	9.8	10.3	10.4	10.4	10.0	9.8
Standardised[4]	8.6	7.2	6.8	8.8	10.0	10.3	10.3	10.4	10.0	9.8
Youth (under 25)	11.8	8.3	8.1	12.8	15.2	15.8	15.7	16.0	14.7	..

1. All figures relate to the United Kingdom. The work force is the sum of employees in employment, the self-employed, H.M. Forces, the participants in work-related government training programmes and the unemployed. Quarterly data shown are for the months of March, June, September and December. Yearly figures are the averages of these four periods.
2. Excluding Community Programme vacancies.
3. The adjusted series has been restricted to claimants aged 18 and over to avoid breaks in the series due to new regulations in the entitlement of young people to claim unemployment-related benefits from 12th September 1988; it also takes account of past discontinuities to be consistent with current coverage. For a full description see *Employment Gazette*, December 1988.
4. ILO/OECD definition, based on Labour Force Surveys.
Source: Department of Employment, and OECD, *Main Economic Indicators.*

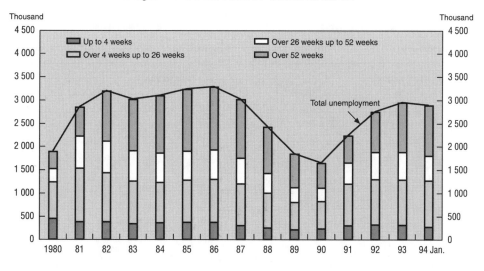

Diagram 7. **STRUCTURE OF UNEMPLOYMENT**

Note: Years are the averages of January, April, July and October figures.
Source: Department of Employment, *Employment Gazette*.

enhancing employment incentives for the former can influence reservation wages generally, as well as giving employers and employees more flexibility. Finally, low entry barriers and the Enterprise Allowance Scheme (1983) encouraged the fastest growth of self-employment in the United Kingdom among OECD countries in the 1980s. Although self-employment was also hit by the recession, it rebounded in 1993, and is now a major source of employment growth.

The cyclical profile of labour productivity has been altered by a shift to quicker hiring and firing practices, with the drop in productivity typically linked to falling output and its subsequent cyclical rebound appearing to be less pronounced. Productivity in this cycle has indeed followed this pattern, except for a surge in late 1992 related to labour shakeout – which with the benefit of hindsight – was based on producers' misperceptions of a further retrenchment of demand and output after sterling's forced exit from the ERM (see Diagram 8, bottom right panel).

25

Diagram 8. **REAL WAGES IN TWO ECONOMIC CYCLES**

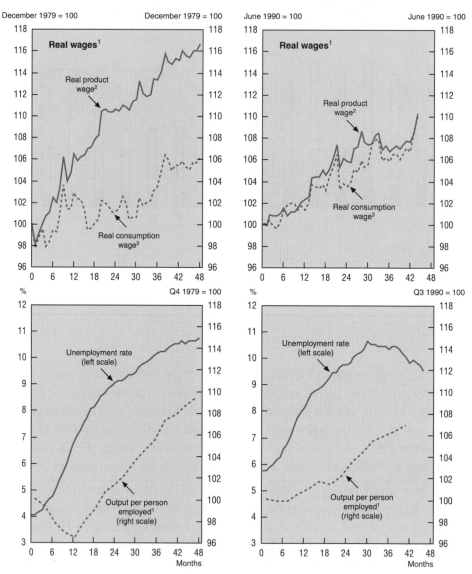

Early 80s cycle

Early 90s cycle

1. Whole economy.
2. Average earnings deflated by the producer price index excluding food.
3. Average earnings deflated by the retail prices index all items.
Source: Central Statistical Office, *Economic Trends;* Employment Department, *Employment Gazette.*

Wage and price trends

At the time sterling left the ERM, the 12-month rate of increase in the RPIX was around 3³/₄ per cent. By March 1994, the rise in the RPIX was some 2.4 per cent (with headline RPI at 2.3 per cent) and might have been even lower in the absence of higher indirect taxes. This degree of disinflation was remarkable. Simulations with the OECD's and other macroeconomic models suggest that the drop in sterling would *ceteris paribus* have boosted the retail price level by some 3 points and inflation by around 2 percentage points after six quarters.[12] In short, had sterling's effective rate remained unchanged, overall price stability or deflation might have prevailed in early 1994.

The effects of depreciation on inflation

Why did depreciation have such muted effects on inflation even allowing for the damping effects of weak world commodity and oil prices? The answer to this puzzle can be classed under three headings:

  i) *Nominal pay and real wages:* Through 1993, pay settlements steadily breached what would historically have been taken as nominal wage floors.[13] Why did pay rises decline following sterling's recent depreciation in contrast to other episodes? In large part, negative price shocks absorbed the initial depreciation price shock and meant that the economy continued on a disinflationary track which proved stronger than anticipated.[14] While nominal pay flexibility has clearly increased, it is too early to say whether this is the legacy of recession or whether the "natural rate of unemployment" has continued to decline in the 1990s after the fall in the late 1980s identified by a number of empirical studies.[15] While real wages increased between 1990 and 1992, this is not particularly surprising given the degree of disinflationary pressure in the goods market and the fact that wages tend to lag behind prices. Real wages started to moderate significantly in 1993 and the wedge between real product and real consumption wages narrowed. This moderation was instrumental in lowering underlying inflation despite depreciation and pricing labour back into work, in stark contrast to the 1980s. Observed wage moderation relative to productivity is not inconsistent with greater real wage flexibility and a further fall in "the natural rate", although it is far from conclusive.[16, 17] Nonetheless, a far greater degree of real wage flexibility may well be needed if unemployment is to be lowered durably in the medium term.

ii) *The output gap:* But, the fundamental factor driving disinflation has been the large output gap, following the tightening of monetary policy in the early 1990s and the process of balance sheet adjustment in the private sector. However, microeconomic reforms pursued since the 1980s have substantially changed attitudes to competition and cost control and have been essential in the emergence of a more flexible and competitive economy.

iii) *Product market competition:* Competition in product markets has in tensified due to both domestic and international factors.[18] Goods prices

Table 3. **Wages and prices**

Percentage changes from the same period a year earlier

	1989	1990	1991	1992	1993	1993			1994
						Q2	Q3	Q4	Q1
Retail prices									
All items	7.8	9.5	5.9	3.7	1.6	1.3	1.6	1.6	2.4
Foods	5.9	8.1	6.3	3.1	2.6	2.7	3.6	2.3	1.5
Producer prices[1]									
Material and fuel purchased	5.3	-1.5	-2.3	-0.2	4.5	6.6	5.6	-0.6	-2.8
Output home sales	4.8	6.3	5.4	3.1	4.0	4.0	4.2	3.8	3.3
Import prices[2]	4.3	2.3	1.2	0.9	8.5	10.2	11.3	1.3	..
Earnings and wages									
Average earnings	9.1	9.8	8.0	6.1	3.5	3.7	3.3	2.7	..
Manufacturing	8.8	9.4	8.2	6.6	4.5	4.9	4.4	4.0	..
Public administration	9.9	10.3	6.8	5.9	4.5	6.1	4.7	2.6	..
Memorandum items:									
National accounts deflators									
Private consumption	5.9	5.5	7.4	4.8	3.5	3.6	3.6	3.2	..
GDP at market prices	7.1	6.4	6.5	4.3	3.4	2.6	3.1	4.4	..
Average price of new dwellings[3]	16.0	5.3	-3.1	-4.4	2.4	2.7	4.2	3.4	..
Unit wage costs[4]									
Total	9.6	9.9	7.0	4.5	0.2	-0.4	0.5	0.5	..
Manufacturing	4.5	7.3	7.0	2.1	0.2	-0.5	1.2	1.6	..

1. Manufacturing.
2. Balance-of-payments definition.
3. Mortgage approved.
4. Wages and salaries per unit of output.
Source: Department of Employment and Central Statistical Office.

were stable or fell in some sectors over the past year. A striking, but representative, example of a general shakeout in the UK distribution system is the retail food sector.[19] In March 1994, the food component of the RPI was up only 0.2 per cent year on year, despite higher prices for imported food products (Table 3).

As in most OECD countries, service price inflation is "structurally" high compared with tradeable goods prices. UK service prices were up less than 4 per cent in early 1994 year on year, compared with over 5 per cent in late 1992. But, increasing exposure of previously sheltered sectors to domestic and international competition (*e.g.* banking, insurance, telecommunications) is accelerating change, as seen by the trend to lower service sector pay, rapid growth of outsourcing and expansion of small businesses.[20]

External trade developments

External trade developments in 1993 were only modestly affected by sterling's exit from the ERM in September 1992. Whereas previous depreciations were typically associated with excess demand conditions, the latest episode was provoked by a conflict for monetary policy between keeping sterling in the ERM and ending the UK's longest post-war recession. The year following depreciation has seen subdued inflation and the nominal depreciation transformed into a large real one. The current account deficit widened only slightly in 1993 as the "J" curve effects – usually accompanying depreciations – proved "surprisingly" absent in the new trade data.

In contrast to recessions in the mid-1970s and early 1980s, the current account remained in deficit throughout 1990-92, reflecting stubbornly high import penetration and a erosion in export performance compared with the late 1980s (Diagram 9). To some extent, this reflected the timing and the level at which sterling joined the ERM in October 1990.[21] Although cost and price competitiveness in late 1990 was in line with the average of the 1980s, sterling appreciated prior to ERM entry, even though inflation was well above that in low-inflation core ERM countries.

Depreciation gradually improved the external accounts in the first half of 1993, despite stagnant Continental European export markets. Export and import prices increased sharply in the first six months, but to a lesser extent in the

Diagram 9. **INTERNATIONAL COMPETITIVENESS FOR MANUFACTURING**

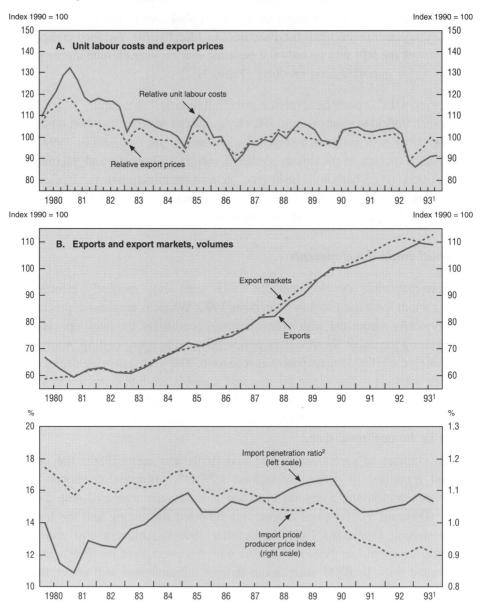

1. Estimates based on total exports for 1993.
2. Ratio of imports of manufactured goods to total domestic demand.
Source: Central Statistical Office and OECD.

second half of the year, as sterling recovered. All in all, the terms of trade improved modestly for 1993 as a whole, in part due to weak world commodity prices. By early 1994, a recovery in sterling led to a further fall in import prices. For 1993 as a whole, the current account deficit remained roughly unchanged at £10.9 billion or almost 2 per cent of GDP (Tables 4 and 5).

The response of trade volumes to shifts in trade prices usually takes several quarters. This time, sterling depreciation was reflected in a pick-up in export

Table 4. **Trade volumes and prices**[1]

Percentage changes

	1988	1989	1990	1991	1992	1993
Export volumes						
Total goods	5.5	8.4	7.2	2.0	1.2	2.9
Food	−0.5	8.1	0.5	5.0	8.6	−1.8
Manufactures	5.1	12.4	7.5	1.8	0.5	−0.5
Energy	−7.8	−19.9	9.3	−0.2	3.3	18.4
Raw materials	−11.6	3.0	−2.2	−9.2	−4.7	11.5
Export prices						
Total goods	−2.2	−5.6	−4.9	0.5	1.0	8.8
Food	1.4	−0.8	7.5	0.6	−3.6	10.5
Manufactures	−1.7	−9.2	−4.4	1.5	2.4	13.3
Energy	−17.3	51.4	10.9	−10.2	−9.3	−11.1
Raw materials	16.3	6.1	−0.5	10.1	7.7	−4.0
Import volumes						
Total goods	16.1	9.5	−0.5	−6.5	7.5	5.5
Food	4.4	2.4	3.1	−0.3	7.5	−1.6
Manufactures	18.2	13.2	−1.0	−9.3	8.3	6.6
Energy	3.1	8.9	9.0	4.0	−1.7	1.0
Raw materials	2.9	0.0	−6.1	−9.3	6.3	4.1
Import prices						
Total goods	−14.4	−7.1	2.0	9.1	−5.8	3.5
Food	−4.6	2.1	4.3	1.0	−6.0	12.4
Manufactures	−16.2	−11.1	3.1	14.9	−5.0	1.9
Energy	−24.1	10.8	4.3	−10.4	−3.1	0.2
Raw materials	0.0	10.3	4.0	2.7	−10.2	4.5
Memorandum items:						
Terms of trade						
Total goods	14.3	1.6	−6.8	−7.9	7.2	5.1

1. On a balance-of-payments basis.
Source: Central Statistical Office, *UK visible trade statistics: review of Intrastat.*

Table 5. **The current account**[1]

£ billion

	1990	1991	1992	1993	1993			
					Q1	Q2	Q3	Q4
Exports	101.7	103.4	107.0	120.8	29.9	29.7	30.6	30.7
Imports	120.5	113.7	120.5	134.5	33.5	33.0	33.8	34.2
Trade balance	−18.8	−10.3	−13.4	−13.7	−3.6	−3.3	−3.2	−3.6
Services, net	5.4	4.0	8.6	7.9	1.5	1.2	2.8	2.3
Investment income, net	1.6	0.3	4.4	2.7	0.0	0.5	1.3	0.9
Non-factor services, net	3.8	3.7	4.2	5.1	1.5	0.7	1.5	1.4
Private transfers	−0.3	−0.3	−0.3	−0.3	−0.1	−0.1	−0.1	−0.1
Official transfers	−4.6	−1.0	−4.8	−4.8	−1.2	−1.1	−1.5	−1.0
Invisibles, net	0.5	2.6	3.5	2.8	0.2	0.0	1.3	1.2
Current balance	−18.3	−7.7	−10.0	−10.9	−3.4	−3.2	−1.9	−2.3

1. OECD definitions.
Source: OECD.

volumes and a slowing in import volume growth in the first half of 1993 (subsequently reversed in the second half of the year). While such developments are consistent with expected price and substitution effects, such quick responses are unusual and recent data should be interpreted with caution. The split between trade price and volume developments may be less reliable than in the past, in part due to the introduction of a new statistical system for recording intra-EU trade. Trade data may thus be subject to future revision.

A feature of recent current-account developments has been the sharp drop in the UK's traditional surplus on invisibles (partly offset by subsequent systematic data revisions). Part of this drop reflects the sharp reduction in net external assets since 1986.[22] These stock data may, however, be largely based on historical cost and understate current market values.

II. Macroeconomic policies and prospects

The stance of macroeconomic policies

The need to rebalance monetary and fiscal policies has become a high priority following the sharp easing in monetary policy in September 1992. The overall stance of macroeconomic policy has been quite expansionary, with the Public Sector Borrowing Requirement (PSBR) in FY 1993/94[23] reaching over 8 per cent of GDP (excluding privatisation receipts) and base lending rates at 5¼ per cent. However, significant tax and expenditure measures were taken to restore medium term budget balance in the two budgets in 1993. A "new" monetary policy framework was also put in place following sterling's departure from the ERM. As fiscal policy is scheduled to tighten steadily and monetary policy is committed to locking in low inflation, the overall stance of macroeconomic policies will tighten considerably from the Spring of 1994 and beyond. Financial and bond market instability in early 1994 underlines the need for maintaining prudent macroeconomic policies to build credibility in the authorities' ability to maintain low inflation and steady economic growth.

The Medium Term Financial Strategy (MTFS)

Since its conception in the early 1980s, a key purpose of the MTFS has been to establish a framework for sound medium-term public finances. Operational guidelines and interpretation of these objectives have evolved importantly. In the FY 1992/93 budget, the objective was to "balance the budget over the medium-term, while permitting the 'automatic stabilisers' to operate".[24] The MTFS was refined in the FY 1994/95 budget to be "to bring the PSBR back towards balance over the medium term, and in particular [as a minimum] to ensure that when the economy is on trend (output) the public sector borrows no more than is required

33

to finance its net capital spending''. This new focus on current and capital spending reflected a concern that budget consolidation not be achieved at the expense of essential investment in public services. The FY 1994/95 budget thus broke new ground in making a clear distinction between current and capital

Table 6. **Budgetary developments**

£ billion

	1991/92		1992/93		1993/94	1994/95
	Budget forecast	Outturn	Budget forecast	Outturn	Budget forecast	Budget forecast
					(November 1993)	
Receipts	230.6	225.8	237.4	224.1	232.0	256.8
of which:						
Taxes on income and oil royalties	79.1	76.2	76.7	72.1	73.9	83.8
Taxes on expenditure	87.0	87.2	93.0	88.2	91.7	100.2
Social security contributions	37.2	36.9	39.1	37.3	39.3	43.3
Gross trading surplus	1.9	1.6	3.7	2.6	3.6	5.0
Community charge/Council tax	7.2	7.1	8.3	8.1	8.0	8.6
Expenditure	241.9	245.4	268.3	269.6	286.5	298.0
of which:						
Final consumption	119.9	126.8	130.9	134.0	140.0	145.2
Subsidies	6.3	6.2	6.1	7.2	7.6	7.3
Current grants to personal sector	70.9	72.0	81.0	82.4	89.5	92.9
Debt interest	17.5	16.8	18.4	17.8	19.8	22.6
Gross domestic fixed capital						
formation	16.1	16.4	18.2	17.6	17.9	16.4
Capital grants to private sector	4.3	4.9	4.1	5.5	5.7	5.5
Unallocated reserve	3.5		4.0			3.6
Financial deficit	11.3	19.6	30.9	45.4	54.5	41.3
Financial transactions	−3.4	−5.7	−2.8	−8.9	−4.8	−3.3
of which:						
Transactions in company						
securities[1]	−5.5	−8.4	−8.0	−8.2	−5.5	−5.7
Public sector borrowing requirement	7.9	13.9	28.1	36.6	49.8[2]	37.9
of which:						
Central government		12.9		36.3		
Local government		1.0		1.4		
Public corporation		0.1		−1.1		

1. Including privatisation proceeds.
2. PSBR outturn for 1993/94 was £45.9 billion.
Source: Central Statistical Office, *Financial Statistics* and *Financial Statement and Budget Report 1991/92, 1992/93,* and *1994/95.*

spending and provided estimates of net capital spending and the public sector's current balance.

The FY 1992/93 budget outturn

The 1992 budget forecast a FY 1992/93 PSBR of £28.1 billion (4½ per cent of GDP), approximately twice the outturn for FY 1991/92 (Table 6). In the event, the outturn was £36.6 billion. This deterioration was mostly in income and expenditure taxes and social security contributions. Tax revenue was weaker than projected, as real GDP was flat in FY 1992/93, compared with a budget time forecast rise of 1¾ per cent. Expenditure outturns were only a little above spending plans announced in the 1991 Autumn Statement. Final consumption expenditure, subsidies and capital grants to the private sector were well above plans, but largely offset by lower outturns for public investment and debt interest. In real terms, however, general government expenditure (GGE) (excluding privatisation proceeds) was up 6.2 per cent, compared with a forecast rise of 3½ per cent – the largest increase since 1974/75. This outcome reflected lower than projected inflation within the context of cash expenditure limits.[25]

The outturn for the FY 1992/93 national accounts financial deficit[26] was £45.4 billion, compared with the £30.9 billion deficit forecast in the 1992 budget. Apart from the revenue shortfalls noted above, the unexpected deterioration was attributable to higher than forecast local authority expenditure and accruals adjustments for lower than expected VAT receipts.[27]

The FY 1993/94 budget

The March 1993 budget was framed with two principal objectives: to permit the nascent recovery to become firmly established; and, to outline specific measures to reduce the structural budget deficit in future years. The measures announced thus had little impact on the PSBR in FY 1993/94 but will have much greater effects in subsequent years. The main measures were:

- the freezing of income tax allowances and the basic tax rate limit;
- the restriction of mortgage interest relief and of the married couple's allowance to a 20 per cent marginal tax rate from April 1994;
- a £500 increase in the income bracket for the lower income tax rate (20 per cent) to £2 500 for FY 1993/94 and a further increase to £3 000 for FY 1994/95;

-   a reduction in the rate of advance corporation tax (ACT)[28] from 25 per cent to 22½ per cent for FY 1993/94 and to 20 per cent from FY 1994/95;
-   a one percentage point increase from April 1994 in National Insurance Contributions (NICs) for employees and the self-employed;
-   the levying of VAT on domestic fuel and power at 8 per cent from April 1994, with the full standard rate (17.5 per cent) applying from April 1995;
-   a 10 per cent increase in road fuel duties, with a commitment to raise them on average by at least 3 per cent in real terms in all future budgets.

These measures were forecast to raise receipts by £0.5 billion in FY 1993/94, £6.7 billion in FY 1994/95 and £10.3 billion in FY 1995/96, compared with an indexed base.

Given these measures and expenditures announced in the 1992 Autumn Statement, the PSBR was forecast to increase to £50.1 billion (£55.6 billion excluding privatisation proceeds) in FY 1993/94, some 8 per cent of GDP. This sharp forecast increase in the PSBR was largely attributable to government expenditure. The New Control Total (NCT)[29] – which excludes cyclical social security,[30] debt interest and accounting adjustments (to national accounts concepts) – was forecast to grow in real terms by 2¼ per cent in FY 1993/94, despite public sector pay rises being restricted to 1½ per cent. Expenditure categories forecast to expand rapidly included social security, education and health, reflecting existing programmes as opposed to new initiatives.

The FY 1994/95 budget

Fiscal consolidation was stepped up in the November 1993 budget. It was also the first budget to unify expenditure and revenue decisions. Compared with previous spending plans, the NCT was cut by £3.6 billion for FY 1994/95 and £1.5 billion for FY 1995/96. These plans imply that the NCT is set to decline by 1¼ per cent in real terms in FY 1994/95 and to rise by 1 per cent in FY 1995/96. For FY 1996/97, the plans provide for real growth in the NCT of 1 per cent. The main measures taken to reduce the NCT were:

–   freezing of government departments' running costs (including pay) and of the wage bills of public sector organisations with delegated pay-authority at broadly 1993/94 levels over the next three years;
–   tighter means-testing of invalidity benefit and making employers fully responsible for paying statutory sick pay (with an exemption for small companies);[31]
–   savings on defence, housing and transport programmes.

It was also announced that unemployment benefit and income support paid to people of working age would be replaced from April 1996 by a Job Seekers Allowance (JSA). A contributory element of JSA will only be paid for the first six months of unemployment (compared with 12 months for the current unemployment benefit). From then on, as with the Current Income Support, payment of JSA will be subject to a means test. These changes are expected to reduce cyclical social security outlays by £0.3 billion in FY 1996/97.

Expenditure saving announced in this budget did not come at the expense of public sector investment, unlike the experience in the 1980's. General government gross investment is programmed at over 2 per cent of GDP, compared with an average of 1.9 per cent of GDP over the 1980s (Diagram 10). Assuming a replacement-cost-depreciation rate of 2 per cent, this level of gross investment should be sufficient to stabilise the general government's capital stock (at replacement cost) to GDP ratio at around 50 per cent, compared with more than 80 per cent in the early 1980s (Diagram 11)[32].

Further large tax increases were also announced. These fall almost entirely on the household sector and were forecast to raise £1.7 billion in FY 1994/95, £4.9 billion in FY 1995/96 and £6.1 billion in FY 1996/97, compared with an indexed base. The main measures were:
–   a lengthening of the freeze on income tax allowances and the basic (i.e. middle) income tax rate limit;
–   restricting the value of the married couple's allowance and of tax relief for mortgage interest to 15 per cent from April 1995;
–   introduction of a 3 per cent tax (which was subsequently reduced to 2½ per cent) on most insurance premiums and of an air passenger duty;
–   an increase in the commitment to increase road fuel duties, to an average of 5 per cent in real terms in future budgets;

Diagram 10. **GENERAL GOVERNMENT GROSS INVESTMENT**
As per cent of GDP

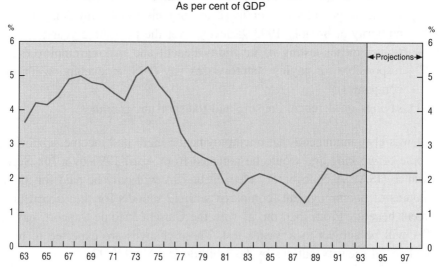

Source: Central Statistical Office, *Financial Statistics;* and OECD.

Diagram 11. **GENERAL GOVERNMENT CAPITAL STOCK[1]**
As per cent of GDP

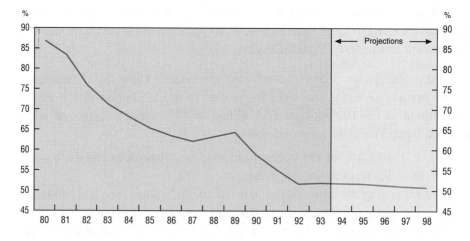

1. At replacement value. This series is affected by the transfer of assets from the general government sector to the private sector.
Source: Central Statistical Office, *Blue Book;* and OECD.

–   to increase duty on tobacco on average at least 3 per cent in real terms in future budgets.

These measures were forecast to reduce the PSBR from an estimated £50 billion (7¾ per cent of GDP) in FY 1993/94 to £21 billion (2¾ per cent of GDP) in FY 1996/97 (Table 7).

The actual outturn in FY 1993/94 was a PSBR of £45.9 billion (7¼ per cent of GDP), an undershoot on the November Budget forecast of £3.9 billion. Of the three components of the PSBR:

–   central government borrowing was £2.3 billion lower than forecast, mainly reflecting lower departmental outlays, down £1.7 billion in total;
–   local authorities' borrowing was £2.0 billion lower than forecast, due to higher than expected capital receipts and improved collection rates of council tax and community charge arrears;
–   public corporations' borrowing was £0.4 billion higher than forecast.

Many of the factors causing this undershoot appear specific to FY 1993/94 and on balance, these lower outcomes are not expected to alter fiscal positions in subsequent years.

Table 7.   **The public sector borrowing requirement**[1]

£ billion

	1992/93	1993/94	1994/95	1995/96	1996/97
General government expenditure[2]	261.1	281[3]	292	312	324
General government receipts	223.3	230[3]	252	280	301
General government borrowing requirement	37.7	46.6	39	32	23
Public corporations' market and overseas borrowing	–1.1	–0.7	–1	–2	–2
PSBR	**36.6**	**45.9**	**38**	**30**	**21**
Percentage of GDP	6.1	7¼	5½	4¼	2¾
Privatisation proceeds	8.2	5.4	5½	1	1

1.   Rounded to the nearest £ billion from 1993/94 onwards.
2.   Figures include NCTs (rounded to the nearest £ ½ billion from 1993/94 onwards) of: 1992/93 232.3; 1993/94 244½; 1994/95 251½; 1995/96 263; 1996/97 272½.
3.   1993/94 outturn data for general government expenditure and general government receipts are not available. Figures given are 1994/95 budget forecasts and are therefore inconsistent with lines below.
Source: Central Statistical Office, *First release (94) 79* and *Financial Statement and Budget Report 1994/95.*

The stance of fiscal policy

Fiscal policy has played an important counter-cyclical role over the past few years. The general government financial deficit rose from 1.3 per cent of GDP in 1990 to 7.7 per cent in 1993, with the sharpest increase in 1992, when the recession reached a trough and monetary policy was constrained by sterling's participation in the ERM (Diagram 12).

The OECD estimates are that cyclical factors accounted for roughly two-thirds of the deterioration in financial positions over the 3 years to 1993. These estimates are subject to a large degree of uncertainty and are sensitive to alternative assumptions on potential and actual output growth and relevant revenue and spending elasticities. Large past fiscal stimuli will be reversed over the next 3 to 4 years. The general government financial deficit is projected to fall to 4.3 per cent of GDP in calendar 1995 (the last year for OECD-short-term projections), almost entirely due to non-cyclical factors – indeed, the cyclically-adjusted-

Diagram 12. **THE STANCE OF FISCAL POLICY**

Change in net lending,[1] % of GDP

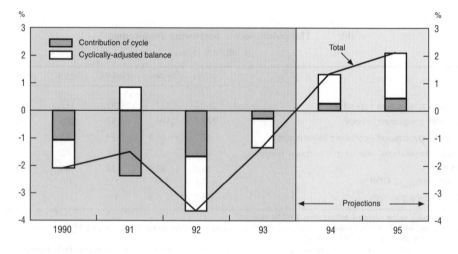

1. General government.
Source: OECD, *National Accounts,* and estimates.

40

budget deficit is projected to decline by around 3 per cent of GDP between 1993 and 1995.

Fiscal prospects

An illustrative medium-term path of the economy is presented in the latest Medium Term Financial Strategy (MTFS) (Table 8). Output growth averages around 3 per cent a year and inflation remains subdued. On these assumptions, and given current policies,[33] public finances are projected to improve sharply over the next few years. The public sector current balance could swing from a deficit of 6½ per cent of GDP in FY 1993/94 to balance in FY 1997/98, while the PSBR is projected to reach approximate balance one year later. As a percentage of GDP, receipts are projected to rise from 36½ per cent of GDP in FY 1993/94 to 40¼ per cent in 1997/98, while current expenditures decline from 42¾ per cent of GDP to 40¼ per cent of GDP over the same period.

Table 8. **The public sector's finances**[1]

Per cent of GDP

	1993/94	1994/95	1995/96	1996/97	1997/98	1998/99
Receipts[2]	36½	37¾	39¼	39¾	40¼	40¾
Current expenditure[2, 3]	42¾	42¼	42	41	40¼	39½
Current balance[2]	**−6½**	**−4½**	**−2¾**	**−1½**	**–**	**1¼**
Net capital spending[2, 4]	2¼	1¾	1½	1½	1½	1½
Financial deficit[2]	8½	6	4¼	2¾	1½	¼
Privatisation proceeds and other financial transactions	¾	½	–	–	–	–
Public sector borrowing requirement	7¾[5]	5½	4¼	2¾	1½	¼
Memorandum items:						
Real GDP growth	2	2½	2¾	3	3	3
Inflation						
RPIX[6]	3	3½	3	2½	2¼	2
GDP deflator	3¼	4	3¾	2½	2¼	2

1. Constituent items may not sum to totals because of rounding.
2. Figures on a national accounts basis.
3. Includes depreciation of fixed capital.
4. Gross capital spending net of depreciation and capital transfer receipts.
5. Outturn estimated at 7¼ per cent of nominal GDP.
6. Percentage change in year to 1993 Q4 and 1994 Q4; percentage change on previous financial year thereafter.
Source: Financial Statement and Budget Report 1994/95.

Fiscal consolidation should bring to an end the rapid increases in public debt as a percentage of GDP. Gross general government debt is projected to peak at 51 per cent of GDP in 1997 (it reached a trough of 34½ per cent of GDP in 1991) and to decline thereafter (Diagram 13). Public sector net debt is expected to peak at a lower level.

Such projections are sensitive to alternative growth assumptions. With 0.5 per cent higher growth on average, the PSBR would reach zero by FY 1997/98, with a surplus of 2 per cent of GDP the following year (Table 9). Were output growth to be 0.5 per cent lower, there would still be a substantially lower PSBR, but it would only fall to 2 per cent of GDP by FY 1998/99. Nonetheless, debt stabilisation would also be achieved, with gross general government debt peaking at 52 per cent of GDP in FY 1996/97.

An important uncertainty in the projections is the likely effects of the freeze on departmental running costs and on wage bills in the rest of the public sector. As wage costs comprise some 75 per cent of departmental running costs, there is limited scope for granting pay increases which are not offset by efficiency gains

Diagram 13. **GENERAL GOVERNMENT GROSS DEBT**
As per cent of nominal GDP

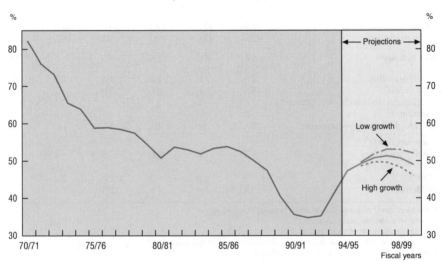

Source: Financial Statement and Budget Report 1994/95.

42

Table 9. **Variant PSBR projections**

Per cent of GDP

	1994/95	1995/96	1996/97	1997/98	1998/99
Higher growth	5¼	3½	1¾	–	–1½
Lower growth	5¾	4¾	3¾	2¾	2
Memorandum items:					
Real GDP[1] growth					
Higher	2¾	3¼	3½	3½	3½
Lower	1¾	2¼	2½	2½	2½

1.   Non-oil GDP.
Source: Financial Statement and Budget Report, 1994/95.

or lower staffing levels. In the rest of the public sector (which has delegated pay authority, *e.g.* National Health and Education) pay increases must theoretically be offset by job losses.

For the freeze on pay bills to be effective, pay settlements will have to be held down or savings achieved to offset higher pay. It would be unrealistic to expect "real" public sector pay to decline to the extent necessary to achieve this result alone: public sector pay might need to decline by 10 per cent in real terms over the four years to FY 1996/97 and more relative to private sector pay (Diagram 14). Instead, the main adjustment is expected to come from higher efficiency gains and savings in government running costs. There is no freeze on pay settlements. Pay determination will proceed normally to ensure recruitment, staff retention and motivation, within the limits of overall expenditure controls. The public sector is expected to deliver efficiency gains comparable to those in the private sector (of at least 2 to 3 per cent a year). Greater emphasis on performance related pay will also help government departments and agencies to maintain public services, while meeting specific targets of improving quality of service.

In the event of slippage, government expenditure would be £0.5 billion (net of tax) higher for each 1 per cent increase in public sector pay. If public sector pay were to increase by 2 per cent per annum over the three years to FY 1996/97, government expenditure in that year could be some £3.1 billion higher than

Diagram 14. **PUBLIC AND PRIVATE SECTOR EARNINGS**

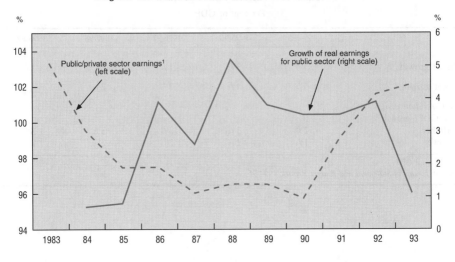

1. Average gross weekly earnings in public services expressed as a percentage of average gross earnings in the private sector. Data are for employees whose pay was not affected by absence.
Source: New Earnings Survey Database.

Diagram 15. **GENERAL GOVERNMENT EXPENDITURE**[1]
As per cent of nominal GDP

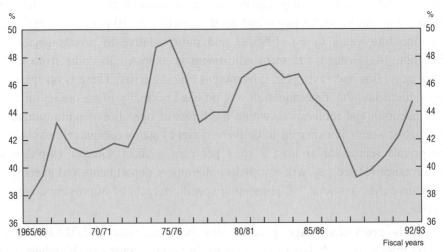

1. Excluding privatisation proceeds.
Source: Financial Statement and Budget Report 1994/95.

44

projected. On the other hand, with above trend output forecast over this period, planned expenditure on social security is likely to be lower[34] (Box 1).

Uncertainty about public sector pay outcomes may be one reason why independent forecasters are somewhat less optimistic on medium-term PSBR prospects. An average of 12 independent forecasts of the UK economy shows the PSBR falling to £24 billion in FY 1996/97, compared with H.M. Treasury's

---

Box 1. **Trends in public expenditure**

The trend rise in general government expenditure (GGE) (excluding privatisation proceeds) witnessed during the 1960's and 1970's ended in the 1980's (Diagram 15). GGE (excluding privatisation proceeds) fell from 46.6 per cent of GDP in FY 1980/81 to 42.1 per cent in FY 1991/92 (two years at a roughly comparable stage of the economic cycle). This reduction occurred despite big increases in social security and health expenditure (the two largest expenditure programmes: Table 10). These increases were more than offset by a reduction in debt interest payments and slow or negative real growth in other programmes. Policy initiatives which reduced growth in other programmes included the ''right to buy'' programme in housing, which encouraged council tenants to purchase their houses, disengagement from the previous widespread system of support and subsidies for industry and, since the mid-1980s, real cuts in defence spending.[36]

Growth in real GGE (excluding privatisation proceeds) since the early 1980s masks important differences between the earlier part of this period and recent years (Table 11). Real GGE (excluding privatisation proceeds) grew at an annual rate of only 0.8 per cent between FY 1982/83 and FY 1988/89 , but by 3.1 per cent per year from FY 1988/89 to FY 1992/93 . This pick-up occurred despite a significant decline in debt interest payments – the increase in real programme expenditure was even greater, rising from 0.6 per cent per year to 4.0 per cent between the two periods. Growth accelerated in virtually all programme categories.[37] Most of this growth was unrelated to cyclical factors. (Social security is the only expenditure item directly affected by unemployment.) But even adjusting for direct unemployment effects, growth in social security outlays was still 3 per cent a year over FY 1988/89 to FY 1992/93 (compared with an unadjusted 5.6 per cent per year).

Part of the acceleration in expenditure in recent years reflects the end to a series of one-off initiatives in the late 1980's and a consequent return of GGE (excluding privatisation proceeds) to underlying trends. In addition, pressure to support economic activity during the latter part of sterling's participation in the ERM (and the 1992 general election) may have eased expenditure constraints. Allowing for the size of expenditure categories, the main sources of potential spending pressures are social security and health.

Table 10. **Programme spending FY 1980/81 to 1991/92**

Per cent

	Share in total GGE[1] 1980/81	Share in GDP 1980/81	Average annual real growth	Share in GDP 1991/92	Change in share of GDP	Share in total GGE[1] 1991/92
Social Security	22.3	10.4	3.7	12.1	1.7	28.7
Health	13.0	6.1	2.9	6.5	0.4	15.3
Defence	10.5	4.9	0.3	4.0	−0.9	9.4
Education	11.8	5.5	1.6	5.1	−0.4	12.1
Total four largest	**57.6**	**26.9**	**2.5**	**27.7**	**0.8**	**65.5**
Trade, industry, energy and employment	4.3	2.0	−0.9	1.4	−0.6	3.4
Housing	5.2	2.4	−5.7	1.0	−1.4	2.3
Agriculture	1.5	0.7	−0.3	0.5	−0.4	1.3
Law and order	3.7	1.7	4.9	2.2	0.5	5.3
Transport	3.9	1.8	0.9	1.6	−0.3	3.7
Other[2]	8.4	3.9	0.9	3.4	−0.5	8.1
Total programme spending	**84.6**	**39.4**	**1.9**	**37.8**	**−1.6**	**89.6**
Debt interest	10.5	4.9	−2.4	2.9	−2.0	6.9
Accounting adjustment	4.9	2.3	−1.8	1.5	−0.8	3.5
GGE[1]	**100.0**	**46.6**	**1.1**	**42.1**	**−4.5**	**100.0**
Memorandum item:						
GDP growth			2.3			

1. General government expenditure excluding privatisation proceeds.
2. Overseas services and aid, other environmental services, National Heritage, miscellaneous.
Source: Treasury Bulletin, 1993, and updates by national authorities.

projection of £21 billion.[38] This difference is only marginally accounted for by divergent growth forecasts: the independent forecasters' real GDP growth projections are virtually identical to the Treasury's until FY 1996/97 (in which year they diverge: the independent forecasters project 2.7 per cent growth, compared with Treasury's assumption of 3 per cent). Differences may reflect the independent forecasters' average views that the favourable effects of growth on the PSBR and the reduction in the structural deficit may be smaller than officially assumed. Notwithstanding a somewhat less optimistic outlook, projected deficit reduction is nevertheless substantial and debt stabilisation is also achieved.

Table 11. **Real growth in programme spending, sub-periods**

Per cent per annum

	1978/79 to 1982/83	1982/83 to 1988/89	1988/89 to 1992/93
Four largest	**3.7**	**1.5**	**4.0**
Social Security	5.0	1.8	5.6
Health	3.6	2.6	4.5
Education	0.4	1.5	3.5
Defence	4.4	−0.4	−0.9
Other programmes	**−0.4**	**−1.7**	**4.2**
Housing [1]	−15.1	−7.4	10.9
Law and order	5.5	4.4	5.6
Transport	2.3	−3.2	9.3
Trade, industry, energy and employment	4.9	−4.6	−4.4
Other	−1.0	−0.2	3.8
Total programmes	**2.3**	**0.6**	**4.0**
Debt interest	3.7	−0.2	−6.6
Accounting adjustments	−3.9	8.7	2.2
Total general government expenditure [2]	**2.3**	**0.8**	**3.1**
Average annual GDP growth	**0.4**	**4.0**	**−0.2**

1. Figures are net of housing receipts.
2. Excluding privatisation proceeds.
Source: Treasury Bulletin, 1993, and updates by national authorities.

Monetary and exchange rate developments

Since September 1992, the authorities have successfully established a new monetary policy framework to replace the ERM's previous role as a nominal anchor. This framework is based on targeting underlying inflation and increasing the transparency of policy decisions (see Box 2). Under these arrangements a quarterly independent assessment of inflation prospects is made by the Bank of England, based on a wide range of real and monetary indicators. Monetary policy is based on an assessment of the inflation outlook within the context of the government's inflation targets.

Short-term interest rates in the United Kingdom have dropped by almost 10 percentage points since late 1990, and until early 1994 long-term rates also fell. Base rates fell from 10 to 8 per cent in the two months after sterling's exit from the ERM, and by January 1993 rates had been cut to 6 per cent. Rates were held there until just prior to the November 1993 unified budget, when they were reduced to 5½ per cent. In contrast, Continental European short-term interest rates began to fall slowly from early 1993, and the earlier large uncovered interest rate differential against sterling narrowed progressively (Diagram 16). This trend, plus sustained UK economic recovery and planned fiscal consolidation, underpinned sterling. During 1993 and so far in 1994, sterling has been broadly stable, fluctuating in a fairly narrow range (Diagram 17).

The authorities continue to monitor narrow (M0) and broad money (M4). For M0, the year on year growth rate edged up to 5.5 per cent in February 1994, compared with its monitoring range of 0 to 4 per cent, although this stronger growth in part reflects adjustment to lower interest rates. In contrast, the year-on-year rise in M4 was 5.6 per cent in January 1994 (monitoring range of 3 to 9 per cent), but might have been higher in the absence of restructuring of corporate

Diagram 16. **INTEREST RATES DEVELOPMENTS**

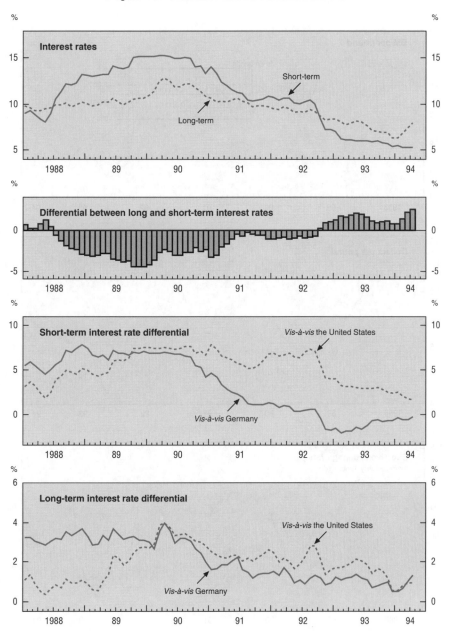

Source: Central Statistical Office, *Economic Trends;* and OECD, *Financial Statistics.*

Diagram 17. **EXCHANGE RATES**

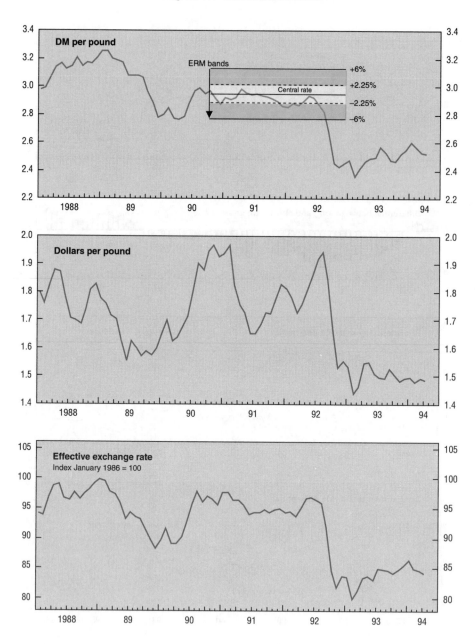

Source: OECD.

balance sheets (Diagram 18). Asset prices and the exchange rate are also closely monitored for indications of emerging inflation pressures.

During 1993, base rate reductions took place against the background of greater disinflationary pressures and stronger output growth than generally antici-pated. Indeed, the Bank of England revised down its inflation forecast quite significantly, as did most independent forecasters. Against a background of falling money market rates, there was a massive portfolio switch into higher yielding longer maturity debt world-wide, especially in the second half of the year. Notwithstanding a very high PSBR, the rally in UK long-term gilts (govern-ment bonds) was exceptional, with spillovers on equity prices. As a consequence, long rates dropped slightly more than short rates and the "yield curve" shifted down during the second half of 1993. Financial market based inflation expecta-tions fell to levels well below cyclical lows in the 1980s (Diagram 19, lower panel) and real indexed yields also fell during 1993, reflecting lower perceived risk.

Diagram 18. **MONETARY AGGREGATES**
Annual growth rates

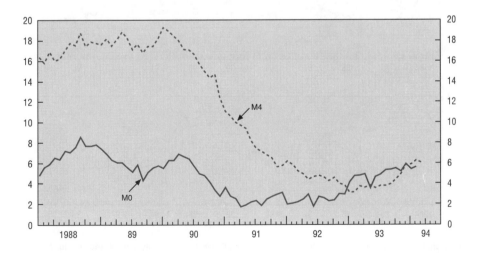

Source: Central Statistical Office, *Financial Statistics.*

Diagram 19. INFLATION AND INFLATION EXPECTATIONS
Year-on-year percentage changes

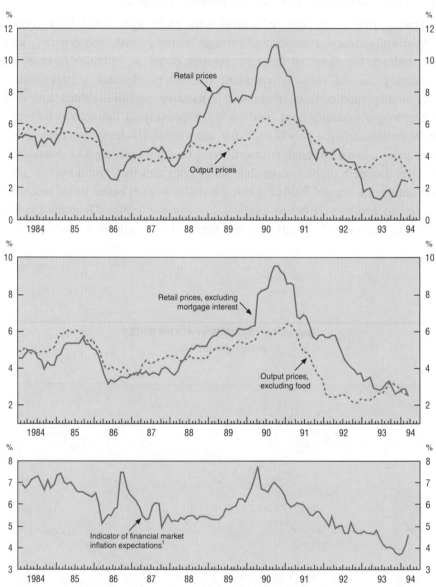

1. Measured by the difference between the real gross redemption yield on Treasury index-linked long-term bonds and the gross yield on Treasury bonds.
Source: Central Statistical Office, *Economic Trends* and *Financial Statistics*.

Early 1994 saw a radical shift in world financial market sentiment. The bond rally stopped in the United States in October 1993, but continued until early January in Europe. On 4 February 1994, the Federal Reserve raised its discount rate by $1/4$ percentage points to $31/4$ per cent. The US rate change came against a background of stronger than anticipated real growth and a mild rally in commodity prices. Fears that inflation pressures might rekindle in the United States and prospects for a slower than anticipated drop in Continental European short term rates triggered a sharp world-wide bond market sell-off in late February and early March. Long-term yields rose sharply in volatile futures-related trading.

In the United Kingdom, a further $1/4$ percentage point cut in base rates to $51/4$ per cent on 8 February 1994, coming against a background of a pick-up in monetary growth and expectations of steady growth in the real economy, was badly received by financial markets. Sterling which had weakened from its mid-January peak against the Deutschemark dropped further. Long-term bond yields which had been edging-up following the firming of US bond rates started to rise steeply. In the space of a few weeks, United Kingdom (and European) long rates rose about $11/2$ percentage points, bringing them back to their levels in late 1993, and the spread between short and long rates widened steeply. Financial markets have since calmed, but real yields on indexed bonds and financial market inflation expectations have also risen.

UK long term bond yields have risen since February by rather more than yields in Germany and the United States, although the differential remains low by recent historical standards. This may suggest that the government's monetary policy framework has not yet gained full credibility in the market, even though inflation has been brought down to the middle of the government's 1 to 4 per cent target range.

Monetary policy is still the responsibility of the Chancellor of the Exchequer and is executed by the Bank of England. In developing its monetary policy framework, the government has concentrated on increasing the transparency of the policy formulation process. Over the last eighteen months the government has made a number of significant steps in that direction. The recent decision to publish the minutes of the monthly meetings between the Chancellor and the Governor is particularly noteworthy in this context. If credibility is enhanced by these moves, current institutional arrangements should contribute to locking in low inflation. OECD projections point to inflation remaining near the mid-point of the government's target range. However, the acid test will only come once the economy approaches trend output, when pre-emptive action will be required to sustain low inflation.

Recent volatility in UK bond markets appears largely to reflect a world-wide shift in investor mood. In part, the recent jump in world long-term bond yields appears to be a correction for overshooting in late 1993. Should inflation expectations and long-term yields remain significantly higher, this will have consequences for the setting of monetary policy and for the real economy in the coming years, even though the UK economy appears to be less sensitive to shifts in long-term rates than other EU countries.

Short-term economic prospects

The economic outlook over the coming two years sketched out below is based on the usual technical assumptions:
- monetary conditions will remain sufficiently firm in the coming two years to keep the rise in RPIX close to the mid point of its 1 to 4 per cent target range;
- the government's tax and spending programmes will be broadly adhered to, leading to a steady reduction in the structural budget deficit;
- nominal exchange rates remain unchanged from their levels of 10 May 1994, slightly below their levels in November-December 1993;
- oil prices average $13.20 a barrel in the first half of 1994 and remain unchanged in real terms thereafter;
- growth in UK export markets for manufactures are in the range of 6 to 7 per cent over the coming two years, picking-up in line with the recovery in economic activity in Continental Europe.

Forces acting

The main forces acting on the economy over the coming two years will be the pronounced shift from public to private sector sources of demand. Large tax increases and slow growth in public spending will reduce the contribution of the public sector in total domestic demand. But improved private sector balance sheets should neutralise these effects, leaving GDP growing at around 2³/₄ to

3¼ per cent – above the growth of potential output. Enhanced fiscal consolidation is timely and will promote a more balanced economic recovery, by moderating the relatively buoyant growth of private consumption and public spending and "crowding-in" business investment and exports.

The main factor sustaining recovery will be the effects of the previous substantial easing in monetary policy. Whereas short rates might drop slightly, in the event of further rapid and substantial drops in Continental European rates, the scope and need for further reductions is limited – the more so if inflation is close to or past its cyclical low.

Against this background, private consumption growth is projected to slow in the face of the rise in taxation in early 1994, but to grow at an underlying rate of 3 per cent thereafter, bolstered by a pick-up in employment and confidence and a slight rise in house prices and household wealth. Business investment typically picks up at this stage of the cycle and there are indications that plant and equipment investment intentions are responding to rising capacity utilisation, and better balance sheet positions and cash flow. The trough in non-residential investment may also have been passed. Once the recovery in Continental Europe begins, improved UK cost competitiveness should help to boost exports, although the foreign balance may deteriorate slightly over the coming years.

Unemployment is projected to come down only gradually to around 9 per cent by 1995, partly on account of rising labour force participation in response to better employment prospects. Although the RPIX will rise in the coming year, due to indirect tax increases, nominal wage growth is expected to remain subdued, albeit picking-up slightly in response to firming labour markets and wage drift. Given low world commodity and energy prices and good productivity gains, the cost positions of firms are expected to remain under firm control. Continuing economic slack could thus hold the rise in private consumption and GDP deflators below 3 per cent over the period to the second half of 1995 – close to or marginally above the mid-point of the government's inflation target range (Table 12).

The trade balance is projected to deteriorate modestly in the coming year on account of buoyant import growth, but exports should pick up in 1995 on the back of improved export order books and the expected recovery in Continental Europe. The invisible balance could also deteriorate slightly, although the current account deficit might still remain close to 2 to 2½ per cent of GDP.

Table 12. **Short-term projections**

Percentage changes from previous period

	1993	1994	1995
Volume (1990 prices)			
Private consumption	2.5	2.8	3.0
Government consumption	−0.5	1.4	1.7
Gross fixed investment	0.8	3.6	5.3
Public [1]	1.6	−4.1	1.8
Private	0.6	5.9	6.1
Final domestic demand	1.6	2.7	3.1
Stockbuilding [2]	0.4	0.6	0.3
Total domestic demand	2.0	3.3	3.4
Exports	3.1	5.7	6.9
Imports	3.5	7.0	7.3
Foreign balance [2]	−0.2	−0.5	−0.3
GDP	**1.9**	**2.8**	**3.2**
Memorandum items:			
GDP deflator	3.4	3.2	2.5
GDP at current prices	5.4	6.1	5.7
Real personal disposable income	1.5	1.0	1.8
Personal saving ratio [3]	11.5	9.9	8.8
Private consumption deflator	3.5	2.9	2.9
Employment	−1.3	1.2	1.4
Unemployment rate [3, 4]	10.3	9.6	8.9
Manufacturing production	1.9	2.8	3.9
Current balance			
£ billion	−10.9	−14.3	−16.5
As per cent of GDP	−1.7	−2.1	−2.3

1. General government and public corporations.
2. Changes as per cent of GDP in the previous period.
3. Data in levels.
4. Unadjusted claimant count.
Source: OECD estimates.

By end-1995, the UK economy could be experiencing the favourable situation of output growth above the growth of potential, with low actual inflation, and falling unemployment – albeit still above the "natural rate". The current account deficit could still be of manageable size albeit rising, and the PSBR on a steadily declining path.

The risks surrounding this projection appear evenly balanced over the short term. The main uncertainty is whether inflation is likely to remain in the mid-range of the government's target band towards the end of this Parliament as cyclical slack is taken up. Higher output and higher inflation cannot be ruled out, but the effects of wide-sweeping microeconomic reforms and the marked drop in inflation expectations make a rekindling of inflation unlikely in the coming two years. Indeed, the acid test will probably only come beyond the forecast horizon, as the economy re-attains trend output. In the interim, prudent monetary and fiscal policies are essential to building credibility in the authorities' ability to sustain low inflation and steady economic growth.

III. The reform of the UK health service: a preliminary assessment

Introduction

Roughly three years have passed since a number of important reform measures were introduced to the UK National Health Service (NHS). These reforms sought to increase the flexibility and efficiency of the system and to enhance the quality of health care. They attempt to accomplish this by creating market-like competition for purchasing and providing certain types of hospital and community health services.[38] This chapter first puts UK health spending in an international perspective and describes the characteristics of the UK health-care system. The key elements of the reform are then presented and the main changes in the system since the reform discussed. Finally, the chapter evaluates what remains to be done in light of how the system has evolved to date in response to the reforms.

UK health care spending: international comparisons

In 1992, the United Kingdom spent £42 billion on health care, representing 6.7 per cent of trend GDP (Table 13). This compares with an average share of health spending in GDP of 8.2 per cent in the OECD as a whole in 1992, and 7.5 per cent in the European Community. As in many other OECD countries, particularly outside North America, the UK ratio of health spending to GDP generally stabilised in the first half of the 1980s following significant growth in the 1970s. Since 1985, this ratio has increased by nearly 1 percentage point of GDP, with relatively strong growth – above the EC and OECD averages – apparent since 1990.

UK health outcomes appear, for the most part, to be comparable with those achieved in other countries. Data on perinatal and infant mortality, and on

Table 13. **Total health expenditure as percentage of trend GDP**

	1970	1975	1980	1985	1990	1992
United States	7.2	8.1	9.3	10.5	12.3	13.5
Japan	4.6	5.5	6.7	6.5	6.9	7.1
Germany	6.0	7.9	8.7	8.5	8.6	9.1
France	5.9	6.8	7.7	8.2	8.9	9.2
Italy	5.3	5.9	7.1	6.9	8.2	8.4
United Kingdom	4.4	5.4	5.9	5.8	6.3	6.7
Canada	6.9	7.1	7.4	8.4	9.3	9.9
Average of above countries	5.8	6.7	7.5	7.8	8.7	9.1
Australia	6.1	8.1	7.8	8.3	8.2	8.4
Austria	5.4	7.2	8.2	8.0	8.6	8.9
Belgium	4.0	5.7	6.7	7.1	7.7	7.9
Denmark	6.1	6.3	6.8	6.4	6.2	6.4
Finland	5.9	6.4	6.7	7.4	8.4	8.5
Greece	4.1	4.0	4.4	4.9	5.3	5.5
Ireland	5.6	8.0	9.3	7.9	7.0	7.1
Netherlands	6.1	7.3	8.1	7.7	8.3	8.7
Norway	5.0	7.2	6.6	6.6	7.3	7.9
Portugal	3.1	6.1	6.2	6.6	6.6	6.5
Spain	3.7	4.8	5.8	5.5	6.9	7.1
Sweden	7.3	8.0	9.6	9.1	9.1	8.6
European Community	4.9	6.2	7.0	6.9	7.3	7.5
OECD total	5.4	6.6	7.3	7.4	7.9	8.2

Source: OECD.

potential years of life lost[39] are close to G-7 and OECD averages; the same is true of life expectancy at birth and at age 80.[40]

Annual growth rates over the last two decades in per capita health expenditures are shown in Table 14. During the 1972-82 period, growth in real health spending (using the GDP deflator) was 3.8 per cent per year, below the EC and OECD averages, but volume growth (column C) moved closer to the OECD average when account is taken of the slightly slower growth in health prices compared with economy-wide prices in the United Kingdom. In 1982-92, real growth in health spending (based on the GDP deflator) was the same as in the preceding decade (but above the EC and OECD averages). However, the rate of increase in "volume" terms was half that of the 1972-82 period, reflecting the fact that "excess" health price inflation grew by 1.7 per cent per year, a relatively strong rate when compared both with the 1970s and with most other

Table 14. **Growth rates of per capita health expenditure**

Annual growth rates

	1972-82				1982-92			
	A	B	C	D	A	B	C	D
United States	12.4	4.1	3.3	0.8	8.6	5.1	2.5	2.7
Japan	14.2	6.6	7.4	-0.7	5.5	4.3	3.3	1.0
Germany	9.8	4.8	4.0	0.7	5.4	2.4	2.4	-0.1
France	16.2	4.8	6.5	-1.7	8.0	3.2	4.3	-1.1
Italy	22.5	4.5	4.8	-0.3	12.9	4.4	3.4	1.0
United Kingdom	18.4	3.8	4.0	-0.2	9.5	3.8	2.1	1.7
Canada	13.5	3.7	3.1	0.6	7.7	4.1	2.7	1.4
Average of above countries	15.3	4.6	4.7	-0.1	8.2	3.9	3.0	0.9
Australia	16.0	3.9	2.8	1.1	8.5	2.4	2.6	-0.2
Austria	13.4	6.7	4.3	2.4	6.6	3.1	1.4	1.7
Belgium	15.5	7.8	7.3	0.5	6.7	2.7	1.8	0.9
Denmark	12.5	2.2	2.9	-0.7	5.9	1.6	1.6	0.0
Finland	16.3	3.9	3.9	0.1	9.9	4.3	2.0	2.2
Greece	21.4	3.4	3.2	0.2	21.1	3.3	3.4	-0.1
Iceland	50.5	6.1	5.3	0.8	26.3	1.9	1.9	0.1
Ireland	20.7	5.2	6.6	-1.3	5.9	1.7	-0.7	2.5
Luxembourg	13.6	5.4	7.0	-1.6	7.5	3.7	2.5	1.2
Netherlands	10.8	3.5	1.4	2.1	3.9	2.2	1.7	0.5
Norway	14.9	4.8	4.6	0.1	8.4	4.3	2.4	1.9
Portugal	..	..	..	..	20.8	3.6	5.0	-1.4
Spain	21.3	4.4	4.6	-0.2	13.1	4.5	5.8	-1.3
Sweden	14.5	4.0	3.2	0.9	6.9	0.1	0.5	-0.4
Switzerland	8.3	3.4	1.5	1.9	6.2	2.4	2.2	0.2
New Zealand	16.8	3.3	..	..	9.9	1.7	1.3	0.4
European Community	16.6	4.5	4.8	-0.2	10.1	3.1	2.8	0.3
OECD total	16.2	4.4	4.2	0.2	10.1	3.2	2.5	0.7

A. Nominal growth in per capita health spending.
B. Real (GDP deflator) growth in per capita health spending.
C. Real (medical price deflator) growth in per capita health spending.
D. "Excess" health price inflation: *i.e.* Medical price deflator less GDP deflator. It should be noted that medical price inflation is generally measured as the difference between nominal expenditure growth and volume growth. In calculating volume growth of health services, an assumption of zero productivity growth is normally made. There are many indicators (reduction in hospital stays, increases in throughput and the introduction of new technology) which suggest that productivity has improved in many countries. The implication is that the volume of health services has risen faster than suggested in column C and that medical inflation is less than in column D. For evidence on the United Kingdom, see Diagram 21.
Source: OECD.

countries during the 1980s. Medical health price inflation does not generally take account of productivity gains. As there is some evidence of a recent improvement in productivity in the United Kingdom, at least, the volume deceleration may be exaggerated.[41]

International differences in levels of per capita health spending appear to be linked closely to differences in overall income or spending levels.[42] Diagram 20 shows per capita health spending related to GDP per capita, where national currency units have been converted to a common currency (US dollar) using GDP purchasing power parities (PPPs). The regression line, which "explains" 78 per cent of the inter-country variation in per capita health spending, suggests that UK health spending per capita is around 14 per cent below its "predicted" level, and substantially below countries such as Australia, Finland, and the Netherlands with similar levels of GDP per capita.

The picture almost certainly changes in the UK's favour when international differences in the prices of medical inputs are taken into account. Tentative estimates of PPPs for health care suggest that the level of UK prices are substan-

Diagram 20. **HEALTH SPENDING VERSUS GDP, 1992**

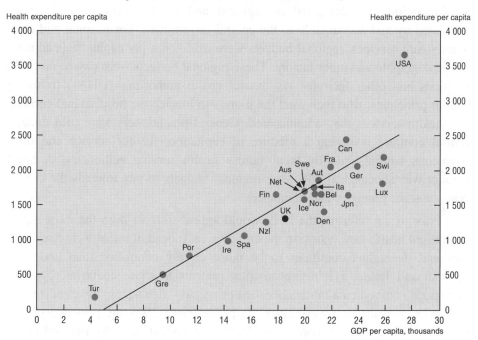

Note: Data shown are PPPs in US dollars, converted to a price level OECD = 100.
Source: OECD, *Purchasing Power Parities and Real Expenditures,* and *OECD Health Systems Facts and Trends.*

tially below the OECD average, while, for example, US prices are significantly above this average. The NHS has several institutional characteristics that have tended to be associated with slower rates of growth in health spending internationally, and which may have helped to produce a lower price structure in the United Kingdom compared with countries with markedly different health systems.[43] It is not clear at this stage whether taking account of relative health prices accounts for some or all of the difference referred to above.

The NHS before reform

The UK National Health Service emerged in broadly its present form in 1948. Although there have been significant reforms to administrative practices at various times, the essentials of the 1948 scheme remained unchanged for several decades. It was paid for almost exclusively out of general taxation. The Secretary of State was accountable to Parliament for all policy and expenditure. Day-to-day administration was delegated to regional and local bodies, but they were appointed by and accountable to the central government. For hospital and community care services, regional budgets were made on a per capita basis adjusted for demographic and other factors. These regional budgets were passed on to the hospitals and other facilities *via* district health authorities (DHAs) following similar principles, who then used the money to finance the hospital and community health services they administered. General practitioners were paid under a central contract involving a mixture of capitation, fee for service and other payments, administered by local family health service authorities. A small amount was allocated to GPs from regional budgets to pay towards the cost of practice staff, premises and computers.

Prior to the reforms, the NHS would appear to have been the most highly centralised health care system in the OECD area. Indeed, it remains more centralised and its budget continues to be more closely controlled than under the Spanish and Italian systems, even after reforms in those countries. The UK system also embodied a much cherished principle – free access by all citizens to comprehensive medical care. Over the period since 1948 the principle of free access had been eroded, notably in dental and optical care. By the end of the 1980s such services were charged at near cost, although people over pension age, pregnant women, children, people on low incomes and those with certain medical conditions do not pay. Pharmaceuticals prescribed by family doctors also carried a charge. Yet visits to the doctor and all hospital care and community health services were free of charge.

The UK pattern of health service delivery is broadly similar to those in Canada or the Scandinavian countries, the main difference being that administration and finance in these latter countries were more decentralised. The UK system differs from some continental European systems (such as those of France and Germany) in that it is not based on an insurance scheme that reimburses secondary service providers on a fee-for-service basis. Prior to 1991, hospitals in the United Kingdom (as in most public hospitals elsewhere) received a budget from central government and had to keep within it. If they do not, the responsible managers might be dismissed or otherwise sanctioned, as has sometimes happened. These constraints and sanctions now apply to the district health authorities as purchasers. This capacity to set and to enforce a budget limit distinguishes the UK system from those of other countries where there are many social insurance agencies and many providers and where budgetary or expenditure control is often ineffective.[44] Tight budget control under the National Health Service, however, was obtained through an inflexible system for allocating funds to hospitals and was frequently associated with long queues and with a lack of sensitivity to patients' needs and tastes.

The other important cost saving feature of the UK system is the family doctor or GP. GPs are paid a fixed amount per patient (depending on age) together with certain allowances and fees for services in return for providing (loosely-defined) general medical services for their patients. Patients have a right to choose their GP, but may not have more than one GP at a time. This GP, in addition to providing ambulatory services, acts as a "gate-keeper" for hospital care; that is, he determines whether or not his patients should be admitted to a hospital for non-emergency or "elective" treatment. No hospital will agree to see a patient for elective surgery unless the GP has given the patient a letter of referral.

Nearly the entire British population relies on the NHS for its health care, though private health insurance is also permitted. In the early 1980s the number of privately-insured individuals grew, but later stalled with the recession. In 1988, only about 15 per cent of the population had some form of private health insurance coverage, most of which was for short-term acute hospital care (Propper and Maynard, 1990). On the whole, the NHS system appears to have provided an adequate level of health services for all people who chose to be enrolled in it. Furthermore, the NHS was able to compete effectively with private health services when the prices it charged for its services were set at or near zero. This is admittedly not a very exacting performance standard, but it is not one that all Member countries' public health services have managed to achieve: in some, the costs of queuing and the uncertainty as to the timing and quality of care have made it hard for the public system to compete, even when the system's explicit charges are far lower than those of private alternatives.[45]

There were good reasons to retain the essential features of the NHS. First, it was, and is, considered by much of the population to be one of the most successful of all British social institutions. Dissatisfaction did increase substantially in the 1980s, as the regular surveys of British Social Attitudes show (Jowell *et al.*, 1991). However, "... far from reducing allegiance to the NHS, dissatisfaction appears to fuel demands for extra expenditure and attention" (Taylor-Gooby, 1991, p. 40). Second, the comprehensive access to free medical care provided by the NHS had brought increased equality to the distribution of health care in the decades since the second world war (O'Donnell and Propper, 1991). Third, as the section on international comparisons has shown, the NHS delivered satisfactory health standards for the UK population and was relatively inexpensive (see also Barr, Glennerster and LeGrand, 1988). It was, and is, a remarkably cost-effective institution. Fourth, the incentives to supply excessive medical services inherent in many continental European and US systems of health finance were absent. The UK Government had powerful and effective means of controlling health costs.

Ironically, it was the major strength of the system – the effectiveness of the budget control process – that played an important role in unleashing the pressure for change. Public spending on health grew substantially more slowly in the 1980s than in the preceding decade and a half relative to GDP. Under Mrs. Thatcher's administration, the rate of growth for total public spending grew broadly in line with GDP in the first half of the decade and somewhat less for inpatient care. But growth was particularly slow from FY 1983/84 on, as tight cash limits began to bite (Table 15). These tight limits coincided with a growth in the very elderly population and a revival in the number of births. This, in turn, was reflected in a real decline in spending per head of the cost-weighted popula-

Table 15. **Resources and demands on the NHS Hospital and Community Health Services, 1983-88**

Per cent per annum

	Real purchasing power increase	Increase needed for demographic change	Real net plus/minus
1983/84	0	0.5	−0.5
1984/85	−0.1	0.6	−0.7
1985/86	0.5	1.3	−1.2
1986/87	0.6	0.9	−0.3
1987/88	1.9	1.4	0.5

Source: H.M. Treasury and Department of Health and Social Welfare.

tion and a resource crunch ensued. The experience of the 1980s underscored the limits of a policy of reducing health expenditure while leaving the institutions of health care delivery untouched. It therefore shifted the policy focus toward systemic reform.

The command-and-control system of the NHS lacked flexibility, incentives for efficiency, financial information (and hence accountability) and choice of providers of secondary care. A prominent American health economist has observed that "it is more difficult to close an unwanted NHS hospital than an unneeded American military base" (Enthoven, 1985). Consultants (senior hospital doctors) with lifetime positions in hospitals had little incentive to run a service more efficiently.[46] There was little incentive to use buildings economically as they had always been paid for by the government. More generally, although comparative data for current hospital costs had been published since the early 1950s and speciality costings had been available since 1988, reliable per unit capital costs were generally absent. More important, there was little incentive for managers to act on the results prior to setting up of the "internal" market in 1991 or to identify more efficient ways of using resources. The flexibility of work practices and pay was limited by national pay settlements. Furthermore, patients could not choose other providers of specialist services even if they were dissatisfied.

The reforms

The motivation for the reforms centred on the belief that an alternative system could be devised that retained the advantages of the NHS – universal coverage and effective cost control – while expanding consumer choice and reducing supply-side inefficiencies. With the reforms, the government aimed to preserve free, or almost free, access to health care and to keep tax-based finance, but to use competition between providers of both hospital and clinical services to improve health and increase consumer satisfaction within a tight budget. In short, it wanted to squeeze more out of the system.

The reforms, which were proposed in a 1989 White Paper (*Working for Patients*, UK DoH, 1989) and implemented in 1991, did not alter the financial underpinnings of the NHS. The central idea that underpins the new NHS is the distinction between the purchaser and the provider of hospital and community health services (that is, of specialist services usually provided by hospitals). The providers compete with one another to provide such services by means of contracts with purchasers of health services.

Under the new system, there are two kinds of purchaser, each embodying a different model of purchasing. First and largest are the district health authorities (DHAs). The reforms recast their role from one of organising and providing hospital care to selecting the services required to meet those needs and then contracting with various service providers. A greater role than formerly is attached to identifying the health needs of the district's population. Regional Health Authorities are funded on a formula basis by the central government and in turn allocate resources to DHAs. DHAs are monopsonists in contracting for many hospital services (such as emergency services and other care not contracted for by GP fundholders; see below).

The second type of purchaser is the General Practitioner fundholder. GP fundholders are self-employed primary care doctors who manage a budget which they must use to secure a defined range of hospital and primary care services for their patients. The fundholder's practice receives a transfer of roughly one-fifth of the per capita costs of hospital and community health services (such funds previously went directly to the local health authority). With this the fundholder is able to purchase a variety of services and products, including some surgical treatments, diagnoses, prescriptions and, more recently, community nursing services.[47]

GPs must have practices of more than 7 000 (9 000 up to FY 1992/93) patients in order to be eligible to become fundholders. Despite the voluntary nature of the decision to become a fundholder, the take-up by GPs has been quite rapid, especially in rural and suburban areas. About 26 per cent of the population were covered by such purchasers in 1993, a figure which is expected to rise to a third in 1994. Since GP fundholders ''compete'' with DHAs and private insurers in purchasing certain services (with the areas of competition being defined by health care regulation), the purchasing side of market is now also subject to some competitive pressures.[48]

The GP fundholders have considerable flexibility in managing their practice budgets in order to improve the quality of care and to attract more patients. First, they can influence secondary providers' behaviour and improve the quality of services for their patients. Second, they can use surpluses (which are separate from GPs' personal incomes) to purchase further secondary care services or to expand the range of services they provide at their surgeries. Apart from purely professional motivations, GP fundholders have strong pecuniary incentives to make good use of this flexibility – by improving the quality and range of services offered, they are able to attract more patients to their practice, raising their capitation income.[49] GP fundholders can further increase their incomes by using budget surpluses to employ staff to undertake income generating activities, such as immunisations and health promotion.

On the provider side, the reforms centre on the creation of ''trust'' status for hospitals and on the obligation for all hospitals and community services, regardless of their status, to compete with each other (and in some cases even with private hospitals) for contracts with health authorities, GP fundholders and private insurers in order to earn their incomes. The trusts are public sector organisations enjoying a high degree of autonomy in providing secondary and community health care. When a hospital or other provider becomes a Trust, its assets are transferred to the Trustees. The trusts have their own governing body, but are accountable to the NHS Management Executive, which monitors their financial performance and business plans. Trusts are expected to break even with a required return on assets of 6 per cent. They may employ their staff on their own contracts and terms of service. Trusts may retain unplanned surpluses and are free to borrow within the External Financing Limit (EFL), which is a form of cash limit set by the Treasury on total borrowing for the sector as a whole. By the end of 1994 well over 90 per cent of hospitals will have become Trusts.

Other changes introduced as part of the reforms were aimed at ensuring that health service managers were no longer able to view capital expenditure as a "free good". The previous lack of any incentive structure in the management of the NHS estate had led to under-use and neglect of valuable capital assets. The capital charging system was designed to rectify these problems and to encourage managers to make the most efficient use of their physical resources by recognising that the continuing use of those resources has a cost. The capital charging system is now a major input into business planning and ensures that the revenue affordability of any capital investment is carefully considered in respect of its likely impact on contract prices.

The reforms opened up possibilities to overcome some of the weaknesses of the old NHS. Districts and fundholding GPs can, in principle, exercise the sanction of exit against secondary care providers on behalf of consumers. Trusts have the freedom to employ staff at privately contracted wages and conditions. They and non-trust hospitals will have to pay for their use of capital equipment. The Treasury, however, continues to limit overall public sector borrowing for capital spending for the sector as a whole. Trusts can obtain some additional financing of an equity nature under "the private finance initiative" which allows ventures to be undertaken with private sector partners. There will be no free entry to this sector except by private hospitals (which, for the time being, are a small[50] and largely a separate part of the UK health care system).

Changes since the reforms

The government has not established a comprehensive research programme for evaluating the reforms. The discussion below draws on the available research[51] and on various indicators published by the government. However, information remains partial in many areas and it is as yet difficult to take an overall view. The evidence is discussed under several headings: health spending, information, choice, quality of care and equity. The section then turns to a discussion of the response to the reforms of key actors, *i.e.* DHAs, GPs and hospital Trusts.

Health spending, activity and efficiency

As noted above, the 1991 changes were intended to improve incentives for efficiency and effectiveness so that the quality of patient care is maximised within whatever resources could be afforded. The changes have, in fact, required higher spending. Contracts, rather than vague understandings, require negotiation before the contract is set and monitoring of compliance after. They require information, especially reliable financial information, something which was not produced under the previous system. Many more managers and financial, accounting and contract staff had to be employed. The result was to increase the budget taken by the NHS in the years before and immediately after the reforms were introduced. Indeed, for a period, the NHS budget rose at rates not seen since the 1960s (see Table 16, and Bloor and Maynard, 1993). The Government viewed the increases which accompanied the introduction of the new system, at least partly, as an upfront investment to maintain and improve the NHS's efficiency record. An indicator of efficiency gain has been derived by comparing increases in spending on hospitals and community health services (after adjusting for demography and relative prices) with a global indicator of increases in activity.[52] Diagram 21 shows that, on this basis, there was an increase in efficiency in the health care sector of about 1.2 per cent per annum between FY 1980/81 and FY 1990/91 – though the rate was declining towards the end of this period. Since the reforms, the annual rate of efficiency gain has increased: to

Table 16.   **National Health expenditure control totals**

	Real expenditure (£ billion)	Increase percentage on previous year
1988/89 Pre reform	23.6	–
1989/90 White Paper	23.9	1.3
1990/91 Preparation year	24.9	4.2
1991/92 First year	26.6	6.8
1992/93 Second year	28.3	6.4
1993/94 Third year estimate	29.1	2.8
1994/95 Fourth year plan	29.5	1.4
1995/96 Fifth year plan	29.6	–

Source: H.M. Treasury.

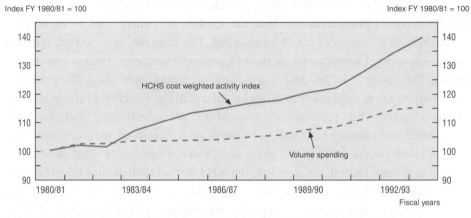

Index FY 1980/81 = 100

Index FY 1980/81 = 100

Fiscal years

1. The cost weighted activity index (CWAI) is a measure of the overall increase in activity in Hospital and Community Health Services (HCHS). It is a weighted average of increases in the main areas of HCHS activity using relative contributions to total cost as weights. Volume spending is defined as HCHS cash spending adjusted for changes in HCHS specific pay and price input costs.
Source: Department of Health.

1.9 per cent in FY 1992/93 with a provisional estimate of 3 per cent in FY 1993/94. The authorities have set a target of at least 2¼ per cent in FY 1994/95. In the most recent public announcements (H.M. Treasury, 1993) health spending is slated to be brought back to the low rates of increase seen in the 1980s.

Associated with the increase in efficiency has been a surge in hospital activity although this – and possibly part of the efficiency gains as well – are not independent of the increase in funding. Total hospital inpatients are estimated to have increased at an annual average growth of 5.1 per cent in the three years since FY 1990/91. In the previous seven years the annual rate of growth was only 2.8 per cent. The reforms have given both purchasers and providers new incentives to substitute day surgery for inpatient care and there has been a sharp rise in day cases. In the three years to FY 1993/94, day cases rose by 16 per cent per annum, a rate more than double that achieved in the seven years before the reforms.

Information on costs and outcomes

The reforms have highlighted the need for improved information and mechanisms to produce it are being put in place. This will inevitably be a slow process. Information on both costs and quality of service is still weak even though: the NHS has produced information on current costs at speciality level since 1988; all clinical work is being fully costed, most of it at below speciality level since the introduction of the internal market; and all GP fundholders and Extra Contractual Referral clinical work is costed by episode of care. Although guidelines for costing were issued when the internal market was created, improvements in costing methodology and clinical consistency are being sought and will be introduced over the next 3 years.[53]

Choice

One of the White Paper's stated intentions for the reforms was to increase patient choice. Patients now have greater freedom to change their GP. In the past, administrative hurdles discouraged patients from changing their doctor. These hurdles have been abolished. Choice remains limited in many rural areas where the density of doctors tends to be low.

A survey has been undertaken comparing the extent to which patients' choice increased in the case of elective surgery referrals in five hospitals in the North West of England (Mahon, Wilkin and Whitehouse, 1994). The authors conclude that the level of patient involvement was low in 1991 and remained low in the first year of the reforms. Only one in ten patients reported being given a choice of hospital. Only one in twenty patients had been offered any choice of consultant. Two-thirds did not know to whom they were being referred, although this did not, in fact, seem important to people. Nine out of ten patients said they were happy with the way the choice was made.

From the patient's perspective, then, the reforms do not yet appear to have expanded consumer choice significantly. While information is scant, patients of fundholders do not appear to have noticed any increase in alternatives presented to them.

GPs' views of how the reforms have affected their choices are somewhat mixed. Three-quarters of all GPs thought that the reforms had made no difference to the choices available, 17 per cent thought it had made things worse and only

5 per cent thought there had been an improvement. Fundholding GPs, on the other hand, appeared to be more sensitive to the range of choice available. They were more likely to believe there was a viable choice of hospital for their patients and more thought that such factors as waiting times were important for their patients (Mahon *et al.*, 1994).

Quality of care

As yet, there has been no broad-based effort to study the impact of the reforms on the quality of care. One study of elderly people discharged from hospital in 1990 and 1992 (Jones, Lester and West, 1994) found little significant improvement in the quality of non-clinical hospital services. In this study it was found that patients waited longer for treatment, on average, in 1992 than in 1990 (even though there was progress made nationally during some of this period). Fewer received information about their hospitals before admission. There were no improvements in food quality or in hospital cleanliness. On the other hand, there were signs that ward staff were trying to improve communication and there was some improvement in the notice patients were given of admission. Ironically though, patient dissatisfaction on this score rose, illustrating a central dilemma for the service: expectations by users are rising all the time, ahead of resources.

Almost no research has been undertaken on Trusts so it is difficult to see whether the Trust status as such is making any difference to the quality or effectiveness of health care. There is much anecdotal and some survey evidence that individual Trusts are making use of their freedom to innovate and improve services (Smee, 1993). In 1992, a survey of eight Trusts covered 900 patients who visited the hospitals before and after they became Trusts. 48 per cent said services had improved, 44 per cent said there had been no change and 8 per cent said they had deteriorated (Department of Health, *Government Response to First Report from Health Committee 1992-93*, CM, 2152, HMSO, 1993).

Since the reforms waiting lists have grown but the average waiting time has declined (for those having to wait at all) from an average of 7.6 months in April 1991 to 4.8 months in December 1993.[54] In-patient waiting lists remained fairly stable over the 1980s, falling in the first years of the decade, then rising and stabilising at about 700 000 from the mid-1980s onwards (Bloor and Maynard, 1993). From 1987, day cases were included in the figures. In September 1987 the total number of cases on the waiting lists in England was 848 000. By September 1993 the figure was 1 030 000. Much of the increase was in day cases.

As part of a "Patient's Charter" the Government has pledged that no one should wait more than two years for inpatient or day care and no one should wait more than 18 months for a hip or knee replacement or for a cataract operation.[55] A central waiting fund was established in 1987 and £250 million used to help reduce waiting times. By March 1993, all regions had eliminated waits of over two years. Waits of over a year had also fallen. Whether this constitutes the best use of money is debatable: targeting the neediest cases on the waiting lists rather than reducing overall average waiting times might be a better approach (Gudex *et al.*, 1990).

Recent national attitudes surveys (Social and Community Planning Research, 1994 forthcoming) suggest some increase in satisfaction with the way in which the NHS is run, both among recent users of the service and among the population as a whole. The same surveys also point to a decline in public dissatisfaction with particular aspects of NHS hospital services since the late 1980s.

The reforms encouraged other measures – for example, the medical audit – to help doctors improve their own standards of care through systematic peer review procedures. A study shows that clinicians did respond quite rapidly (Kerrison, Packwood and Buxton, 1994). The audit process that was studied, however, involved consultants and their juniors and rarely any other professional group. The main method used was a retrospective look at case notes and there was very little consideration of cost, health gain or consumer satisfaction. These weaknesses are now being addressed. An independent evaluation of the audit programme has been established and a high profile national committee, the Clinical Outcomes Group, has been set up to advise on fuller development of clinical audits.

Equity

Though not explicitly stated as a goal in the Government's White Paper, equity and equal access are deep in the public's perception of what the NHS is there to deliver. In the past forty odd years since the Service was created, it has succeeded in reducing the inequalities in the distribution of GPs and hospital resources between regions. Regional differences in ages at death have declined steadily, at least until the mid-1980s (Whitehead, 1987; Townsend, 1990; Klein, 1991; LeGrand, Winter and Woolley, 1990). The North-South divide in mortality has disappeared over the last fifty years for younger age groups, though it remains for older ones (LeGrand and Illsley, 1991, and forthcoming). Will the 1991 changes reverse this pattern of improvement?

The United Kingdom has had one of the most sophisticated and effective means of allocating health resources to areas of need. This is a complex area with important lessons for other OECD countries. From 1976 to 1991 allocation of the health budget to regions was based on a formula – actually different formulae for England and Wales, Scotland and Northern Ireland – which reflected the different needs or health status of the population treated in those areas. Under the reforms, the allocation formula was revised. The new regional formula is age-weighted (as was the previous one) but contains lower weight on mortality rates. However, some regions have kept the previous weight on mortality and some have intro- duced allowances for social deprivation into their formulae for districts. What was arguably more important, was that after the reforms, allocations were made from regions to districts (now purchasers) for their resident populations rather than for the hospitals they contained. The new formula suggests that parts of the south east of England (a relatively prosperous region, but containing areas with elderly populations) need more resources, relative to areas which on other criteria appear to be more deprived. The basis for drawing up the national formula is now being reviewed once again using new data on morbidity from the national population census. The abolition of regions (from April 1996) makes it likely that any new formula will be applied directly to districts.

One of the most persistent concerns has been that the existence of GP fundholders as a separate (and more effective) group of purchasers is creating a two-tier service in terms of the quality of care. During the initial stages of the reform, it was the large and well organised practices in suburban and rural areas that first took advantage of the scheme. As the spread of fundholding progresses these differentials may widen because the quality of service received by those registered with fundholding GPs has improved; the very success of fundholders as purchasers may widen the gap between the quality of services received by their patients and that received by others. It must be emphasised, though, that wide variations in the standard of general practice already existed in the pre- reform National Health Service. The answer to the potential inequity is not to abandon this effective form of purchasing but to extend fundholding and GP-based purchasing to cover more patients and this is happening.

Response of key actors

DHAs as purchasers

At the outset, in 1991, most hospitals remained "district managed units", but nearly all hospitals will have Trust status by 1994. The reforms seem to have clarified DHAs' role as purchasers and to have freed them from having to manage such day-to-day problems as nurse grading reviews, labour disputes and detailed purchasing requirements. It has left hospitals and other providers with a clear mandate to manage themselves. It has also focused districts' attention on thinking about local health needs and priorities (Klein and Redmayne, 1992).

For a number of reasons, however, the split between purchasing and providing services – that is, between the DHAs and the local hospitals – is not yet always very sharp and the districts' purchasing function remains underdeveloped. First, in many districts, a single dominant provider traditionally maintains close links with the DHA and its officials.[56] This may weaken competitive pressures in local health care markets. The long-term possibilities of competition should not be dismissed, however. One study of contracting in the West Midlands, the largest region in the country (Appleby et al., 1994) concluded that about a quarter of the hospitals were in a pure monopoly situation, but that others did face a potentially competitive situation. Second, district officials tend to avoid the political embarrassment likely to follow from decisions not to contract on a large scale with the local hospital. Third, many districts have continued to rely heavily on providers in hospitals to tell them what is needed.[57] Contracting skills are at a premium in the DHAs and the detailed medical knowledge required to bargain on equal terms with a hospital consultant in his or her specialty is often absent. Those in charge of contracting are often inexperienced and poorly equipped to do the job.

General practitioners as purchasers

The aim of the GP fundholding scheme was to give "GPs an opportunity to improve the quality of services on offer to patients, to stimulate hospitals to be more responsive to the needs of GPs and their patients and to develop their own practices for the benefit of their patients".[58] Within the range of services that they are permitted to purchase, GPs do seem to have done a better job of purchasing than DHAs. GP fundholders have been more prepared to diversify providers, to challenge hospital practices and to demand improvements. GPs are closer to patients than DHAs and hear more about their complaints. GPs have the medical knowledge and status needed to confront hospital doctors in contracting. In short, with GPs as purchasers, the information balance is better, though still far from equal. They also have the motivation to contract on patients' behalf (Glennerster *et al.,* 1994). There is considerable logic to more GP-based purchasing (Audit Commission 1993).

On the other hand, GPs do suffer from a number of competitive disadvantages compared to DHAs. They are less well informed about broader public health questions, such as where to place accident and emergency centres in order to minimise the response time to motor accidents. Since they are small relative to DHAs, transactions costs may be higher for some types of contracting. The optimal boundary between purchasing activities that are solely the responsibility of the DHAs and those in which GP fundholders are allowed to compete is still being tested.

One part of the reforms clearly has begun to show concrete results. GP fundholders are given a cash-limited sum to spend on the drugs they prescribed (in addition to the budget for purchasing hospital care described above). If the GP spends less than this amount the surplus can be used for other treatment. This direct incentive, which applies only to fundholders, has not significantly reduced the cost of prescribing, but it has slowed the rate of increase in fundholders' costs compared to non-fundholders. This is true nationally and in two control trials of fundholders and non-fundholders (Bradlow and Coulter, 1993; Maxwell *et al.,* 1993). The fundholding GPs look more carefully at new and costly drugs and tend to use more generics.[59] In FY 1992/93, the national increase in prescribing costs was 12 per cent but the fundholders' increase was only 8 per cent.

Hospitals and Trusts as providers

The new organisational arrangements – trust status and contracting between purchasers and providers – were expected to lead to better performance through devolution of management and through the sharper incentives provided by competition. Initial indications regarding performance of Trusts are encouraging. Most trusts have adhered to financial requirements. Trusts have out-performed other hospitals in terms of increases in the number of patients treated. They have been more successful than other hospitals in reducing the number of patients awaiting treatment for more than one year. These performance comparisons are highly inconclusive, however. Hospitals that opted for trust status – especially those that did so early on – were not a representative sample of UK hospitals. A study by LeGrand and Bartlett (1994) shows that the first hospitals gaining trust status were already the most effective.

In looking at the performance of the new secondary care system, it is necessary to keep in mind the structural context in which these reforms have been implemented. First, the pre-reform NHS was characterised by excess hospital capacity in certain areas[60] and, despite the already-cited downward trend in hospital beds, it remains a problem. Second, with capital costs so much higher, the competitive position of hospitals has been undermined relative to that of doctors' offices and community clinics for treatments that can now be done on an outpatient or day-patient basis. Thus, it is important to assess the impact of reforms by asking whether or not they have enhanced the sectors' capacity to cope with these structural challenges. In this respect, the reforms – by at least opening the door to more flexible financing arrangements and to alliances with other health care actors – almost certainly have been a success, although it is doubtful that they have gone far enough (see below).

Looking ahead

Experience in other areas of policy suggests that shifting from "command and control" to "market-based" systems is not straightforward. In UK health care, the responses of various actors – especially the performance of the GP fundholders – were not entirely anticipated at the time the reforms were enacted. Given the complexity of the sector, unanticipated responses are not unusual, and there will no doubt be further surprises as the market for health services develops over time. By 1996 there will be 80 to 90 DHA purchasers and possibly 15 000 GP fundholders in groups of purchasing consortia. On the supplier side, 450 trusts (fewer, if closures or amalgamation are allowed) are expected in 1996. Within this general context policy makers must continue refining a policy strategy that will discipline spending pressures, maximise efficiency and welfare gains and allow structural change to occur – permitting successful innovations and institutions to take hold and unsuccessful experiments to be eliminated. In the nearer term, a number of specific problems need to be addressed if the reforms are to have their full positive impacts. These are taken up in the following paragraphs.

Structural adjustment in the hospital sector

As a result of political and technological developments, pressures for change are likely to be particularly intense for hospitals. Up to the present, competition has been very limited: contracts have been set to maintain the status quo and purchasers have been instructed to give considerable warning of their intention to take their custom elsewhere. But as competition increases and some hospitals prove more attractive providers than others, some will wish to expand as others contract or close. Rules for exit have not yet been clearly established. Pressures are already appearing in high cost urban areas, particularly in London. The government has stated its intention to reduce beds in inner cities but there is considerable opposition from local interest groups particularly in the London area. In this context, the government has set up the London Implementation Group to find appropriate solutions which go with the grain of the market. It is to be hoped that the decisions will help set the criteria and rules which can guide the development of the market in the future. More generally, the government needs to make it clear that market signals must be heeded if appropriate resource reallocation decisions are to take place.

Hospitals will undoubtedly follow several strategies in responding to structural pressures. Hospital amalgamation, particularly if economies of scale and scope obtain, may be one way to proceed to reduce excess capacity and this is being tried in London. Vertical integration may be an option for hospitals wishing to provide a broader package of services – such as nursing and primary care as well as acute care. At the other extreme, hospitals may find cost savings from increased specialisation in certain areas and – given that patient risks from surgery tend to be lower in hospitals where there are high volumes – there may be strong medical grounds for this. It is not yet clear that the current administrative framework for determining entry, exit, expansion and contraction in the hospital sector will be able to cope with upcoming adjustment challenges. It therefore becomes increasingly important to clarify the ground-rules for such processes in the sector.

Unlike the areas around major cities and in the densely populated south-east of England, some regions may not have large enough patient volumes to support several large hospitals. Indeed, one of the main adjustment challenges for health care policy will be to encourage a service structure that allows such areas to be served in a cost-effective manner. In these circumstances, care should be taken to avoid closing down hospitals without first giving them a chance to explore various survival strategies (*e.g.* through vertical integration). For this to happen, trusts may need to run losses over the short term, something they are not currently allowed to do. Allowing trusts to borrow on private markets may also be an option as long as it is clear that there is no obligation by the government to bail them out. In some sparsely populated areas, though, the market may not be able to support more than one hospital (meaning that it is, in essence, a local natural monopoly). Here, other regulatory mechanisms for pricing may need to be envisaged (similar to those used for public utilities).

Further decentralisation of decision making

In principle, hospital trusts have been given the freedom to manage and to negotiate separate agreements with their employees. In practice, this has been curtailed. The central authorities have been reluctant to permit full decentralisation and have intervened over pay and in a number of operational matters. Ministers have now expressed the clear intention that local pay bargaining should take effect in the coming year's wage round. This process needs to be extended further. Without a clearer separation of roles and a substantial increase in operating freedom, the trusts cannot be expected to produce the hoped-for efficiency gains.

At the same time, trusts will need to tighten control over their own resources. Most have had to take over existing contractual arrangements for labour and very few have tried to modify these in any significant way and then only for new staff.[61] Integrating clinicians – who are key to the production process – into the management of hospitals, has a considerable way to go, even though this was a requirement for obtaining trust status. Wages of hospital doctors are still largely determined centrally and the attribution of distinction awards (which accord large wage increases and form a key role in doctor incentives) is still partly centralised and heavily influenced by the clinicians themselves although there is increasing input from local management. Making the medical staff more accountable for achieving overall goals of the hospital, with the ability to sanction where necessary, is likely to be a key element in achieving efficiency gains.

Some hospitals may wish to invest either to improve the quality of services provided or, where they have proved successful in attracting business, to expand. As it stands, trust hospitals can retain surpluses earned and some narrow scope exists to re-invest them. In addition, there is an overall External Financing Limit for total borrowing for capital expenditure established by the Treasury. The rules for attributing capital, while requiring certain rate of return criteria to be achieved, are still based on administrative rules rather than on market criteria. Hospitals have only limited scope to borrow in private markets, although private equity investment in collaborative arrangements with the private sector is being encouraged under the Private Finance Initiative. Rules in this area may also need to be examined.

Improved pricing practices

Correcting the weakness of the DHAs' contracting capability will require the progressive "unbundling" of contracts in order to permit better comparison of the cost of particular services between hospitals and better monitoring of contracts. This, in turn, means that providers must enhance transparency through better cost accounting and information on outputs so that contract performance can be monitored and evaluated. At the same time greater discretion must be given to hospitals in setting prices. Under current arrangements, hospitals must set prices in line with average costs to ensure that total costs are covered. However, this reduces the scope for competition on the basis of marginal cost pricing as well as for innovation and downward pressures on costs. Hence, it is not surprising that little competition on price has taken place outside of the London area.

Better purchasing co-ordination and better information

The White Paper "The Health of the Nation" (1991) presented the government's health strategy and objectives.[62] It set targets in selected areas and stressed the importance of prevention in achieving them. These goals are to be reflected in the NHS strategies in purchasing health care and other health-related services at the regional and district level. The White Paper proposes an extensive system of consultation and co-ordination to achieve coherent policies affecting health. In its aims, the government would appear to be in the forefront of countries attempting to achieve more coherent health policies which recognise that health care is only one part – albeit an important one – in improving health. The purchaser-provider split provides a means of re-orienting funds towards prevention if this is demonstrated to be more cost effective.

Nonetheless, the government's approach – taken in the context of the NHS reforms – is likely to run up against some difficulties. First, information on the effectiveness of preventive measures is weak, although this problem is not limited to the United Kingdom alone. Much more information is required here. The current GP contract, which now stipulates a number of core services to be provided and financial incentives for a number of preventive measures, is a case in point. For some of these measures, there is little evidence as to whether the financial incentives are cost effective and whether the financial rewards are in line with the expected benefits, although this is critical in establishing more appropriate incentive structures (Scott and Maynard, 1991).

Second, the incentives set up by the current payment arrangements need to be monitored. It is often not easy to recognise poorly structured incentives until the sector has had time to fully adjust to them. The potential problems here are cost shifting, under-serving and "cream skimming". In the case of fundholders, these incentives appear to have been reduced since the budget resources they receive are entirely separate from their practice income.[63] On the other hand, hospitals may attempt to shift some of the cost onto community service budgets of local authorities (home help and residential care), for example, by discharging patients early.

Improved contracting

Intensifying competition in health care crucially depends on the capacity of the DHAs to contract effectively. With a few exceptions, this has been the weakest area of the reforms. GP fundholders proved initially more adept in this area, partly reflecting the fact that their medical knowledge serves to balance the power of hospital specialists. For the DHAs, block contracts were the norm at the beginning as the government attempted to ease in the reforms by maintaining the status quo. Since then, DHAs have become progressively more adept and contracts have evolved although at differing speeds across DHAs. There is evidence of shifts in spending taking place and DHAs are increasingly looking to market test services. Improving the purchasing function in the new internal market is a stated key priority of the government (UK Department of Health, 1993; NHSME, 1993). Since long-standing relationships are likely to be sustained between purchasers and providers for much of secondary care – such as emergency services – the risk of "cosy" relationships continuing or becoming re-established will remain strong.

Here again, though, an important problem facing DHAs is the lack of information. In the past medical priorities were largely determined by the medical corps. More needs to be known about the health needs of the population. While important progress has been made in developing an agreed set of population health outcome measure,[64] further work needs to be done to establish where health care can make the greatest contribution to health status. Likewise, not enough is known about the costs of individual components of health care, so that costs can be balanced against expected gains. Finally, information on the quality and quantity of output provided is often wanting, making monitoring of contracts more difficult. Purchasers will also need to progress further in the evaluation of the appropriateness of the health care provided, ensuring, for example, that it is in line with accepted protocols. This may require increasing the medical expertise within the purchasing agencies themselves. This capacity for evaluation needs to be extended to the general practitioners as well.

Longer-term considerations

It is not yet clear how the new arrangements will affect the long-run development in areas such as medical research and development; human capital accumulation in the sector; and the organisational arrangements by which the various actors – government, teaching and research institutions, service providers and purchasers – co-ordinate these various activities. If the goal of improving information on the effectiveness and cost of different treatments is realised, this will ultimately provide clearer signals for much of the long-term development of the sector. But at the same time, local purchasing practices, which attempt to get best value for money, will gradually erode the possibilities of financing research, teaching and training through cross-subsidisation within hospitals. This may require establishing greater central financing and control specifically aimed at supporting these functions.

IV. Structural issues

Since the early 1980s, the United Kingdom has implemented far-reaching structural reforms aimed at increasing the supply-side flexibility of the economy. Central to this programme has been a strategy of broadening and deepening the influence of market mechanisms wherever possible, while addressing market failures in resource allocation. Reforms since mid-1992 and some evaluative work on earlier reforms are first reported in this chapter. It then examines the financial soundness of the UK's public pension scheme.

Progress in structural reform

Labour markets

Labour-market reform was a key element of structural reform in the 1980s. A major focus of these reforms was to reduce the power of trade unions: employers now have the right not to recognise unions and to bargain directly with individual workers. Measures taken during the past 18 months have built on these reforms. The 1993 Trade Union Reform and Employment Rights Act further restricts the circumstances in which unions can legally hold a strike or other industrial action by requiring seven days notice and by giving members of the public the right to seek injunctions to halt unlawful action depriving them of goods or services. Freedom of choice has been enhanced by giving individuals the right to join their preferred trade union. Trade union members have also been given greater rights in union ballots. There have also been a number of measures which afford employees greater protection against unjust dismissal. Employees have the right to a written statement of their main conditions of employment, and the right for disputes with their employer to be settled by an industrial tribunal. Every employee who becomes pregnant can take a minimum of fourteen weeks maternity leave and is fully protected against dismissal on grounds of maternity.

The Act also abolishes the remaining Wages Councils, which set minimum wages in some industries.

The Government announced in the November 1993 Budget plans to consolidate the present unemployment compensation system, which features various benefits[65], by introducing a single benefit for the unemployed: the ''Job Seeker's Allowance'' (JSA). A contributory element of JSA will only be paid for the first 6 months of unemployment (compared with 12 months for the current unemployment benefit). From then on, as with the current Income Support, payment of JSA will be subject to a means test. JSA will be more efficiently delivered[66] and the link between payment and claimant's job-search activities will be strengthened through a tougher sanctions regime. The new system is expected to encourage more active job-search by the unemployed.

A number of schemes are being piloted with a view to enhancing active labour market measures. There are already schemes offering intensive help to the long-term unemployed and there will be a scheme to allocate an individual Employment Service caseworker to each unemployment benefit claimant to boost incentives to participate effectively in the labour market. In addition, a Jobfinder's Grant, which would assist with the costs of transition from benefit to work, will be piloted.

Invalidity benefit is to be better targeted on those genuinely incapable of work. From April 1995, invalidity benefit will be replaced by a new incapacity benefit, access to which will depend on more objective medical tests. So as to give employers an incentive to manage sickness absences better, statutory sick pay is no longer to be reimbursed to large employers. National insurance contribution rates (NICs) are being adjusted to compensate for this change, so that the net effect is to favour firms with low sickness absences.

To encourage participation in the labour market by those with young children, Family Credit, a benefit for those in work will exclude from the means test an amount of income calculated to cover the costs of childcare. So as to reduce the non-wage costs of employing people on low wages NICs are being further reduced by an average of £2 per week for employees earning less than £200 per week.

Education and training

Education and training reform has been a major focus of microeconomic reform over the past decade. Reforms have aimed to address perceived weaknesses in vocational training, the content of school programmes and participation in post-compulsory education. Although there have been no further significant reforms since the previous Survey, there have been a number of reports assessing progress to date and future directions for reform.

A recently published study[67] highlights what has long been perceived to be the major shortcoming of education and training in the United Kingdom – the failure to equip that part of the population not bound for higher education with vocational qualifications. This shows up in a relatively small proportion of the workforce having craft qualifications (*e.g.* carpenter, plumber, etc.): the proportions of the workforce gaining higher education qualifications (*i.e.* degrees and technical vocational qualifications) are broadly in line with those in the other European countries included in the study (Table 17). It is argued that one of the reasons for the lack of crafts qualifications is that the costs of training are too high due to the poor basic educational attainments of many school leavers. Mathematics tests administered to 13 year olds in a number of countries show UK attainment levels lagging those in other European countries included in the study, particularly for low achievers (Table 18).

Numerous reforms over the past decade have sought to expand vocational education and training. The most important of these are:

– the rationalisation and classification of vocational qualifications into a comprehensive system of National Vocational Qualifications (NVQs) and General NVQs (SVQs in Scotland);
– the establishment of the Youth Training Scheme (YTS) in 1983, which was subsequently enhanced and renamed Youth Training (YT);
– the transfer of the administration of most major government training initiatives (and some employment initiatives) to a network of employer-led organisations, called Training and Enterprise Councils (TECs).

NVQs are designed to attest to competence in jobs while general NVQs provide broadly-based preparation for work and a ladder to higher qualifications; general NVQs are intended to provide an educational route for full time students that is an alternative to the more academic A-levels. Both sets of qualifications are

Table 17. **Vocational qualifications of the workforce**

Per cent of all economically active persons

	United Kingdom 1989	France 1988	Germany 1988	Netherlands 1989	Switzerland 1991
Degrees	11	7	11	8	11
Vocational	25	40	63	57	66
Technical	7	7	7	19	9
Craft	18	33	56	38	57
Non-vocational	64	53	26	35	23

Source: S.J. Prais (1993), *Economic Performance and Education: The Nature of Britain's Deficiencies*, National Institute of Economic and Social Research, Discussion Paper No. 52, p. 9.

earned by demonstrating competence in doing certain tasks rather than knowledge or theory about the subject. This central aspect of the new system has been controversial.[68] Opponents claim that the new system will leave UK crafts persons less skilled than their European counterparts.[69] The lack of rigour in testing has also been criticised.[70] However, NVQs were designed with the needs of industry to the fore. By the end of 1993, ½ million NVQs had been awarded and studies by the CBI and Institute for Manpower Studies (IMS) confirmed their popularity with employers, the practical content of NVQs being one of their

Table 18. **Scores in international mathematics tests, 1990**[1]

	United Kingdom	France	Italy[4]	Switzerland	United States
Arithmetic average	59.5[2]	64.2	64.0	70.8	55.3
Highest decile	89.3	89.3	88.0	93.3	82.7
Lowest decile	32.0[2]	37.3	36.5	50.7	29.3
Relative variability (per cent)[3]	95.0	81.0	81.0	60.0	97.0

1. 13 year old pupils.
2. Adjusted for low response.
3. Difference between highest and lowest decile as percentage of arithmetic mean.
4. Emilia-Romagna only (sample response rate satisfactory at 78 per cent).
Source: IAEP Study, 1990; extracted from Lapointe *et al., op. cit.*, p. 145.

selling points. Moreover, NVQs have the merit of being based on competencies specified by industry.

YT provides vocational education and training, mainly for 16-17 year olds so as to produce better qualified young entrants into the labour market. Training is aimed at a minimum of NVQII level although training below that level is provided for young people with special training needs. About half the qualifications gained on YT are NVQII or higher and three quarters of those completing YT are successful in getting a job, entering further education or being accepted for further training. Within the framework of YT, Youth Credits are progressively being introduced. The Government has announced that by 1995, every 16 and 17 years old leaving school will have the offer of a Youth Credit. The aim is to further increase the proportion of school leavers who participate in training, and within that group, to increase the proportions achieving qualifications at NVQII and above. In addition, the Government has announced a modern apprenticeship scheme for young people from 1995. These are expected to be of three years duration. By 1998, there are expected to be around 150 000 trainees on the scheme, producing some 40 000 NVQIII qualifications each year.

TECs, the employer-led organisations which administer most government financed vocational training schemes, have been assigned three main objectives: organising the training of the unemployed; raising the skill level of the employed; and stimulating enterprise. According to a co recent study, based on survey work between 1990 and 1992,[71] their focus has mainly been on training for the unemployed – they have made little progress towards their other objectives. Nonetheless, the study concluded with positive support for TECs (and LECs) and gave support for their potential. Moreover, recent information suggests that shortcomings highlighted in the report are being addressed. For example, participation in the Investing in People Initiative has doubled since the report was compiled. TECs have accumulated revenue of £230 million available for spending on discretionary programmes, and one-half of Civil Service secondments to TECs have ended.

A number of reforms have also been made to improve the quality of school education. The Education Act 1988 introduced a national curriculum, extensive compulsory testing, open enrolment (giving parents more choice of schools) and allowed schools to opt out of local-authority control and into a system of funding (from the Funding Agency for schools) that allows greater administrative independence. Following substantial opposition from teachers, the Government commissioned a report on the national curriculum and its assessment. The report,[72] published in January 1994, recommends that the national curriculum be reduced to occupy 80 per cent of school time for most children, that it focuses only on core subjects and that testing is only compulsory for these subjects. It is also recommended that schools be allowed to offer 14-16 year olds a wider range of vocational subjects, with time spent on core subjects being reduced to 60 per cent for students doing these vocational courses.

The problems which have been encountered in expanding vocational education and training raise questions about whether this is the best way to raise the educational attainment of the workforce. Concerns about weaknesses in vocational education and training are usually based on comparisons with other European countries, especially Germany. And the solutions are usually inspired by German arrangements. But the United Kingdom does not, and perhaps cannot have the institutional arrangements which make a Germany-type system work. Germany, like other countries where companies play a central role in providing vocational education (through, for example, apprenticeships), has strong and well coordinated business organisations, which enable employers to set national standards; stable shareholdings and long-term bank financing, which reduces pressure to pursue short-term profits at the expense of long-term profits; and national collective bargaining, which reduces poaching.[73] Within this framework, the social partners have well defined roles: employers devote a part of their budgets to training; government provides vocational schools for young trainees; and trade unions moderate wages for new entrants into the labour market.[74] In the absence of these structures, it has been argued that the United Kingdom should seek to exploit the comparative advantage in the structures it does have, which resemble those in other English-speaking countries.[75] This would suggest moving towards the North American route of mass general higher education and accepting manual workers who are less skilled than their German counterparts but more specialised; the concomitant comparative advantage in production would tend to be in services rather than in manufacturing. In fact, there has been a dramatic rise in staying-on rates at secondary school (where courses are largely general) and in participation in higher education: the staying-on rate of 16 year olds has increase from 48 per cent in 1989 to 65 per cent in 1992 and the percentage of 18 year olds going on to higher education has increased from 15 per cent in 1988/89 to 28 per cent in 1992/93.

Taxation

Tax reform has also been a major plank of microeconomic reform over the past decade. A key reform objective has been to reduce distortions in economic decision-making caused by the tax system at times. But raising revenues in ways that are politically least difficult has also influenced tax decisions. As a result, only some of the tax measures taken during the past 18 months (see Chapter II) have continued the drive towards a more neutral tax system and hence, towards greater economic efficiency.

Efficiency aspects of the 1993 tax increases

All taxes except a lump-sum tax distort economic choices[76] and so, in the absence of relevant externalities, reduce economic efficiency. Given that fiscal consolidation called for tax increases, the question arises as to whether those chosen are likely to have the least adverse effects on economic efficiency.

The decisions to freeze income tax allowances and to restrict further mortgage-interest tax relief and married couple's allowance should contribute to improved economic efficiency. Income tax allowances reduce economic efficiency by increasing the marginal tax rates required to raise any given amount of income tax revenue; they also detract from equity because their value is greatest for those paying the highest marginal income tax rates. Mortgage tax relief is also subject to this criticism. In addition, mortgage tax relief (in the absence of taxation of imputed rentals and capital gains) could result in excessive investment in owner-occupied dwellings. The measures announced in the 1993 budgets follow similar measures in earlier budgets.

With respect to the increase in employee National Insurance Contribution (NICs), the effect on efficiency depends on whether they should be considered as taxes or insurance premiums. As most contributory benefits paid by the National Insurance Fund[77] are unrelated to contributions, NICs should generally be regarded as income taxes. Because NICs are capped, they result in an income tax scale inclusive of NICs which is sometimes regressive. For an individual receiving married couples allowance, the sum of the marginal-basic tax rate and Class 1 NICs in FY 1994/95 declines from 35 per cent on annual incomes between

£6 445 and £22 360 (the income ceiling for NICs) to 25 per cent on income up to £27 145 and then rises to the top rate of 40 per cent (Diagram 22). Such a pattern of marginal income tax rates reduces efficiency by calling for higher marginal income tax rates on incomes other than those in the favoured bracket to raise any given amount of revenue; in addition, it does not seem equitable that marginal income tax rates are lower for the favoured income bracket than for those with lower incomes.

The extension of the 20 per cent lowest marginal income tax bracket may have ambiguous effects on efficiency. The measure is costly in terms of lost revenue, necessitating higher marginal income tax rates for many taxpayers to make up for the loss. From an efficiency point of view, the cost of more taxpayers on higher marginal income tax rates is unlikely to be compensated for by the benefits of some low-income taxpayers (those with taxable incomes of £2 500-£3 000) facing a marginal tax rate of 30 per cent (20 per cent plus 10 per cent NICs) instead of 35 per cent.

Diagram 22. **MARGINAL INCOME TAX RATES**[1, 2]

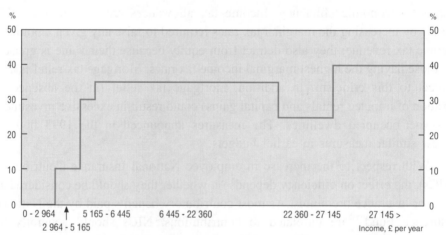

1. Including class 1 National insurance contributions (NICs).
2. Income tax rates and NICs for FY 1994/95. Assuming the following allowances and reliefs: personal allowance £3 445, relief for married couples allowance at 20%.
Source : H.M. Treasury.

The reduction in income tax credit on dividends and the related cut in the rate of Advanced Corporation Tax (ACT) may also affect economic efficiency, although some of the impact will be beneficial. The cut in the tax credit will discourage pension funds and individuals on the 40 per cent rate from investing in equities, but it will also reduce the current tax incentive to pay dividends and use new equity finance rather than retain profits. The cut in the ACT rate (and the introduction of the Foreign Income Dividend Scheme) was designed to reduce the tax bias against foreign investment, and the disincentive to pay dividends, for companies with surplus ACT.

With respect to indirect taxes, the measures announced are generally more likely to enhance economic efficiency. The levying of VAT on domestic fuel and power is desirable even in the absence of environmental externalities as it broadens the VAT-tax base, reducing the VAT rate required to raise a given amount of revenue, and ends the incentive to consume domestic fuel and power in place of goods and services taxed at the standard rate.[78] Allowing for the environmental costs of energy consumption, an indirect tax rate even higher than the standard VAT rate could be justified on efficiency grounds. The move to raise duties on road fuels will improve efficiency to the extent that the environmental costs of vehicle usage are not yet fully reflected in motorists' variable costs. Given that the environmental costs of motor vehicles relate mainly to their usage, the shift in emphasis in vehicle taxation away from fixed costs (such as car excise duty) towards variable costs (such as petrol tax) is to be welcomed.[79] As for the other indirect tax measures, the introduction of an air passenger tax will promote efficiency to the extent that the tax reflects the costs of providing airport services to passengers. Similarly, the introduction of a tax on most general-insurance premiums should enhance economic efficiency by extending the indirect tax base to an activity formerly exempted.

Distributional aspects of the 1993 tax increases

The effects of tax increases (from March 1993 to April 1995) on households by income deciles is analysed in a recent paper by Giles *et al*.[80] They find that around 80 per cent of households will pay more tax and that the average increase in tax will be £10 per week (Table 19). Virtually all households in the upper income deciles will pay more tax. As a percentage of household income, tax increases are greatest on the middle and upper deciles excluding the top decile.

Table 19. **Impact of tax changes 1993-95, by decile group**

Decile	Per cent losing	Per cent gaining	Average gain/loss (£ per week)	Average gain/loss (per cent of income)
1	60	6	–2.1	–2.0
2	38	10	–1.2	–1.1
3	57	7	–2.9	–2.4
4	79	4	–6.0	–3.9
5	91	1	–8.8	–4.5
6	94	1	–11.5	–4.8
7	98	0	–13.0	–4.9
8	98	0	–14.9	–4.7
9	98	0	–16.5	–4.4
10	98	0	–20.2	–3.4
All	81	3	–9.7	–3.9

Source: Christopher Giles and Paul Johnson (1994), "Taxes up, taxes down: the effects of a decade of tax changes", *IFS Commentary*, No. 41.

The general progressivity of the increased tax burdens reflects the increases in income tax and in NICs. The lump sum nature of these increases beyond certain income levels explains the drop in losses at the top decile. The contribution of these tax increases to greater after-tax income equality will partly offset the opposite effect of the tax cuts from 1985 to 1992.[81] However, this analysis only makes partial allowance for social security effects. Assessment of the distributional impact of the budgets needs to consider both tax and social spending.

Financial markets and institutions

In May 1993, the Chairman of the Securities and Investments Board (SIB) published a review of SIB responsibilities under the Financial Services Act. The review's recommendations, which focus primarily on a fresh approach to supervision and enforcement, were supported by the Government. The SIB has since been using its regulatory powers more forcefully. Following a report by the Office of Fair Trading, the Government have directed the SIB to propose new rules for disclosure in the sale of investment-linked insurance products, including rules requiring full disclosure on the cash value of commissions or equivalent. The SIB have published a further discussion paper on the regulation of UK equity markets, in order to ensure that regulation, while robust, does not impede competition. The Bank of England is leading work to speed settlement in the securities markets and to introduce an electronic securities settlement system. The Government will participate, particularly on the legislative implications.

Following the loss of a substantial part of the assets of the pension funds of companies controlled by the late Robert Maxwell, the Goode Committee was established to review pension law. The Committee's report, which was released in late 1993, is currently being considered by the Government. The report proposes to protect pension members through a regulatory system which includes fitness tests for trustees, minimum solvency requirements, a compensation scheme, whistle-blowing powers for trustees and professional advisers, and a new regulator with substantial powers of investigation and enforcement.[82]

Competition policy

Public regulation of utilities has been strengthened by the Competition and Service (Utilities) Act 1992, which brings the powers of all utility regulators with regard to standards of service up to the level of the strongest. The Act includes provisions giving utility regulators powers to set and monitor standards for the utility companies, to facilitate greater competition in the provision of water and sewage services and to resolve disputes between customers and the utilities.

Public sector

Decentralisation of pay bargaining in the public sector has continued. For example, Next Steps[83] agencies can negotiate pay agreements that reflect conditions in their local labour markets. Fifty seven agencies with 200 000 employees have now been established and there are plans for a further 32 covering 30 000 additional employees. Three local authorities have already broken away from national wage agreements. Performance pay is now being extended throughout the Civil Service.

The National Health Service (NHS) has been restructured with the aim of improving the efficiency, quality and cost-effectiveness of public health provision through the introduction of an internal quasi-market (see Chapter III).

The railway system has recently undergone its biggest shakeup since nationalisation. A separate company, Railtrack, has been created to take over the ownership of British Rail's (BR) infrastructure (tracks, signals and stations) from 1 April 1994. Train operations will be progressively transferred to the private sector through the sale of 25 franchises. Bidders for franchises will indicate how much they are prepared to pay, or what subsidy they would require to provide a specified level of service. Franchise holders will lease rolling stock from the three new BR leasing companies which took over BR rolling stock on 1 April 1994, or from elsewhere. Both Railtrack and the BR leasing companies are to be privatised within the next few years.

Infrastructure – the private finance initiative

The Government announced in November 1992 its intention to involve private sector finance and management in a whole range of activities and services traditionally regarded as the exclusive domain of the public sector (for its role in the NHS, see Chapter III). This programme, known as the private finance initiative (PFI), offers the private sector investment opportunities where the private sector genuinely assumes risk. The PFI covers a wide range of areas, but has so far been concentrated in the field of transport infrastructure. Projects were announced in the November 1993 budget to design, build, finance and operate roads by private contractors and to finance privately a new air traffic control centre. The PFI also embraces a number of rail projects to add major rail links to the infrastructure and upgrade existing ones (*e.g.* a new fast rail link between the Channel Tunnel and London, and the upgrading of the West Coast Main Line between London and Glasgow). A panel with members occupying high level positions in the public and private sectors has been set up to promote the initiatives.

Privatisation

Privatisation has continued since the previous survey with the sale of the third and final tranche of shares in British Telecom. The state coal industry will be privatised by January 1995. Public sector bus companies in London and airports in Northern Ireland are to be privatised this year.

Future state-pension commitments

As in other OECD countries, the United Kingdom faces population ageing. The proportion of the population over retirement age is set to increase markedly as the "baby boom" generation retires. Given that state-retirement pensions are financed on a pay-as-you-go (PAYG) basis, these demographic trends raise concerns about the adequacy of future pensions and/or the required contribution rates. This section briefly examines the outlook for the UK's public pension scheme.

The current scheme

Universal (*i.e.* non means-tested and non-occupational) retirement pensions provided by the UK Government have two main components: the basic state pension; and the pension from the State Earnings-Related Pension Scheme (SERPS). The basic state pension is a flat-rate benefit payable to those over the qualifying age (65 for men, 60 for women but to be phased up to 65 between 2010 and 2020) who have paid National Insurance contributions (NICs) for around 9/10ths of their working lives.[84] SERPs is an additional earnings-related pension available to those paying full Class 1 NICs.[85] This scheme was introduced in 1978 and will not pay any full-rate pensions until 1998. SERPs will ultimately pay a pension of 20 per cent of relevant earnings[86] averaged over 49 years (*i.e.* pensionable age minus 16).[87] Both the basic state pension and the SERPs pension are financed on a pay-as-you-go (PAYG) basis from NICs.[88]

Means-tested benefits are also available to those having attained pensionable age; these top up the basic-state and SERPs pensions. Such benefits include income support, housing benefit and council tax benefit. In FY 1991/92, around 15 per cent of pensioners received income support and around one third received some form of means-tested benefit.[89] Benefits to pensioners in FY 1991/92 amounted to £24.7 billion for the basic state pension and £5.8 billion for the means-tested benefits.[90] Means-tested benefits are financed out of consolidated revenue.

The other major sources of retirement pensions are occupational and private pension schemes. Members of occupational or private pension schemes are able to contract out of SERPs; *i.e.* they pay reduced NICs and are not eligible for additional (*i.e.* SERPs) pension.[91] Most occupational schemes are contracted out of SERPs.[92] Around one half of the working population make contributions to occupational pension schemes, as has been the case since the mid-1960's, and a little over half of the population having attained pension age receive occupational pensions. With respect to private pensions, individuals have been able to contract out of SERPs into defined-contribution Personal Pension Plans (PPPs) since 1988. PPPs are now held by around one quarter of the work-force, with take-up having been high amongst the young and much lower for older individuals. This pattern of take-up reflects: *i)* changes to accrual rates which mean that SERPS is presently more generous to older workers (this effect will diminish over time), and *ii)* that the NIC rates is paid at a flat rate, which favours younger individuals (which may encourage some individuals to opt back in when they are around 40 years old).[93]

Demographics

The structure of Britain's population is ageing. The proportion of the population of pensionable age (assumed to be 65 for men and 60 for women) is projected to rise from 18.4 per cent in 1990 to 23.5 per cent in 2030 and to decline slightly during the 2040s (Table 20). Over the same period, the proportion of the population at working ages (16-64 for men, 16-59 for women) is projected to decline from 61.5 per cent in 1990 to 56.6 per cent in 2030 but to recover slightly to 58 per cent by 2050. (The estimates of future pension commitments discussed below assume the current retirement age for women. Allowing

Table 20. **Summary of projection of total population of Great Britain**

Numbers in millions and per cent of total (shown in brackets)

Age group	1990	2000	2010	2020	2030	2040	2050
Children	11.2	12.4	11.8	11.5	11.9	11.4	11.2
(0-15)	(20.1)	(21.5)	(20.2)	(19.4)	(19.9)	(19.3)	(19.3)
Working ages	34.3	34.7	35.3	35.3	33.7	33.6	33.7
(16-64 for men,							
16-59 for women)	(61.5)	(60.4)	(60.6)	(59.7)	(56.6)	(57.0)	(58.0)
Pensionable ages	10.3	10.4	11.2	12.4	14.0	14.0	13.2
(65 and over for men,							
60 and over for women)	(18.4)	(18.1)	(19.2)	(20.9)	(23.5)	(23.7)	(22.7)
Total	55.8	57.5	58.3	59.2	59.6	59.0	58.1
	(100.0)	(100.0)	(100.0)	(100.0)	(100.0)	(100.0)	(100.0)
Number at working ages per							
pension over pension age	3.3	3.3	3.2	2.0	2.4	2.4	2.6

Source: National Insurance Fund Long Term Financial Estimates, 1990.

Diagram 23.   **RATIO OF CONTRIBUTORS TO BASIC RETIREMENT PENSIONERS**

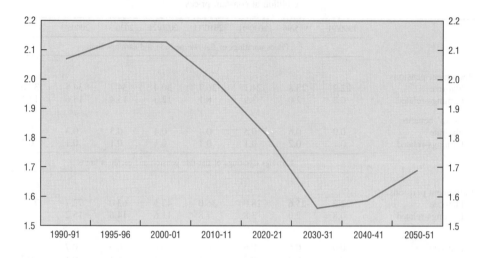

Source: HMSO, National Insurance Fund Long Term Financial Estimates.

for the planned increase in women's retirement age to 65 would reduce estimated future pension commitments.) On the basis of National Insurance Fund (NIF) assumptions about the proportions of the working age population which are economically active[94], these projections imply a decline in the number of National Insurance contributors per flat-rate pensioner from 2.1 in FY 1990/91 to 1.4 in 2030 before rising to about 1.5 in 2050 (Diagram 23).[95] These developments reflect the ageing of the "baby boom" generation.

Future outlays and contribution rates

Estimates of future expenditures on flat-rate and SERPs retirement pensions are provided by the National Insurance Fund (NIF).[96] If the flat-rate pension and the earnings limits continue to be uprated in line with prices, as they have been since 1980, the estimated cost (in 1990 prices) of these pensions rises from £23 billion in FY 1990/91 to around £50 billion over 2030-2040 and then declines slightly (Table 21). On the other hand, were the flat-rate benefit and the earnings limits to be uprated in line with earnings[97], expenditure on retirement pensions would soar, reaching £77.6 billion by 2030 and around £85 billion by

Table 21. **Estimated cost of retirement pensions**

£ billion at constant prices

	1990/91	1995/96	2000/01	2010/11	2020/21	2030/31	2040/41	2050/51
	Prices upratings of flat-rate pension and earnings limits							
Retirement pensions:								
Flat-rate	22.2	23.8	24.1	26.7	30.4	34.7	34.5	32.6
Earnings-related	0.8	2.0	3.9	8.1	12.3	15.4	15.6	14.1
Widows' benefits:								
Flat-rate	0.9	0.6	0.5	0.4	0.4	0.3	0.3	0.3
Earnings-related	0.1	0.2	0.1	0.1	0.1	0.1	0.1	0.1
	Earnings upratings of flat-rate pension and earnings limits							
Retirement pensions:								
Flat-rate	22.2	25.6	28.0	36.0	47.5	63.0	72.7	79.7
Earnings-related	0.8	2.0	3.8	7.8	11.6	14.6	15.2	15.1
Widows' benefits:								
Flat-rate	0.9	0.6	0.6	0.6	0.6	0.6	0.7	0.7
Earnings-related	0.1	0.2	0.2	0.1	0.1	0.1	0.1	0.2

Note: Components may not sum to totals due to rounding.
Source: National Insurance Fund Long Term Financial Estimates, 1990.

the middle of next century. Almost all of the additional expenditure resulting from upratings in line with earnings would be on the flat-rate pension. (These estimates make no allowance for expenditure on means-tested benefits).

It is estimated that, despite population ageing, the main Class 1 joint employer/employee NICs (excluding the NHS contribution) required to finance these pensions under price-linked uprating would fall progressively from 19.1 per cent in FY 1990/91 to around 14 per cent by the middle of the next century (Table 22). The effect on contribution rates of the decline in the number of National Insurance contributors per flat-rate pensioner would be more than offset by growth in real earnings (assumed to be 1½ per cent per annum). On the other hand, were benefit and earnings limits to be uprated in line with earnings rather than general prices, contribution rates would rise markedly, peaking at 26.4 per cent in FY 2030/31 and only declining to 24.5 per cent by FY 2050/51.

Table 22. **Projected Class 1 contribution rates**

Percentage

| Financial year | Upratings and revaluation of contribution limits in line with: | | Assumed contracted-out |
	Prices	Earnings	
1990-91	19.1	19.1	5.8
1995-96	18.1	19.2	4.8
2000-01	17.8	19.9	4.3
2010-11	17.4	21.3	3.6
2020-21	17.8	23.5	3.4
2030-31	18.4	26.4	3.4
2040-41	16.4	25.8	3.4
2050-51	14.1	24.5	3.4

Note: The rates shown are the main Class 1 joint employee/employer contributions for National Insurance (*i.e.* excluding the NHS contribution). The reduced rates for lower earners have been assumed to change in proportion to the main rate and the earnings to which they apply to change in proportion to the earnings limits.
Source: National Insurance Fund Long Term Financial Estimates, 1990.

Retirement pension levels

Were the basic state pension and the earnings limits to continue to be linked to prices, the basic pension for a man on average earnings would fall from 16 per cent of earnings in 1990 to 9 per cent in 2030 and to 7 per cent by the middle of next century (Table 23); for women, the basic pension would fall from 24 per cent in 1990 to 10 per cent in 2050. Additional pension would still rise over the coming decade as SERPs matures, but would steadily decline thereafter. After peaking at 21 per cent of earnings for men (19 per cent for women) in 2000, additional pension would fall to 12 per cent of earnings for men (16 per cent for women) by the middle of next century. The total of basic pension and additional pension at award would decline from 28 per cent of earnings for men (35 per cent for women) in 1990 to 19 per cent (26 per cent for women) by 2050. On the other hand, were the basic pension and earnings limits to be indexed to earnings, the total of these pensions would rise somewhat reflecting the maturing of SERPs.

Conclusions

The United Kingdom is set to experience population ageing, especially in the two decades following 2010. Provided that the basic-state pension continues to be indexed to prices, no increase in NICs will be necessary; this outcome would be even more likely were those currently contracted out of SERPs

99

Table 23. **Pensions at award for men and women on average earnings as a proportion of earnings before retirement**

Percentage

Year of award	Uprating in line with:					
	Earnings			Prices		
	Basic pension	Additional pension	Total	Basic pension	Additional pension	Total
Men						
1990	16	12	28	16	12	28
2000	16	21	37	14	21	35
2010	16	18	34	12	18	30
2020	16	18	34	10	18	28
2030	16	17	33	9	16	25
2040	16	16	32	8	14	22
2050	16	16	32	7	12	19
Women						
1990	24	11	35	24	11	35
2000	24	19	43	21	19	40
2010	24	16	40	18	17	35
2020	24	16	40	15	18	33
2030	24	15	39	13	17	30
2040	15	39	11	17	28	
2050	24	15	39	10	16	26

Note: The table relates to pensions for single persons; for a married couple relying on the husband's insurance the basic pension would be 60 per cent higher. Retirement is assumed to take place on an uprating date and the additional pensions are based on earnings throughout working life at the average level for full-time employees of each sex, without allowance for absence; the benefit levels in the table thus represent the maxima for average earners.
Source: National Insurance Fund Long Term Financial Estimates, 1990.

prevented from opting back in. However, the downside of price indexation is that there would be a substantial fall in the value of this benefit relative to average earnings. In these circumstances, an increasing number of retirement pensioners would qualify for means-tested assistance, necessitating some increase in general taxation. But at least the extent of tax/NICs increases would be minimised by the targeted nature of such assistance. The alternative of indexing the basic pension to earnings would result in substantial increases in NICs and would undoubtedly still require increased general taxation to pay for the rise in means-tested assistance associated with population ageing. This option, which would be extremely costly, has not been followed since 1980 and seems unlikely to be revived.

V. Conclusions

A year and a half ago, when the previous OECD Economic Survey of the United Kingdom was undertaken, macroeconomic prospects appeared highly uncertain. Following the suspension of sterling's participation in the ERM, macroeconomic policy faced the dual challenge of further encouraging economic recovery, while checking the inflationary consequences of sterling's depreciation. This has been achieved to date. Output is now rising steadily, unemployment is falling and underlying inflation has declined.

Economic recovery had in fact begun in early 1992, its profile being dominated by adjustments in household balance-sheet positions and stronger exports. Given extremely high indebtedness at the outset of the recession, sharp drops in interest rates since late 1990 prompted a rapid decline in debt-service payments and were the catalyst to recovery. Short-term interest rates have dropped nearly 10 percentage points since then and, until early 1994, long-term rates also fell.

By the Spring of 1994, the UK economy had reattained its 1990 peak level of output – two years after the start of economic recovery. This same level of output was produced with roughly 1.8 million fewer jobs and greater reliance on female and part-time workers. In marked contrast to other EU countries, UK unemployment peaked at a lower rate in the recession of 1990-92 than in the previous recession. A striking feature was the unusually early drop in unemployment starting in January 1993, with registered unemployment down by 250 thousand by March 1994. To some extent, this outcome can be attributed to labour market reforms and changes in the tax and transfer system in the 1980s, which have promoted modest nominal and real wage outcomes, and more flexible employment practices.

Inflation and inflation expectations have fallen markedly during the past year. By March 1994, the 12-month rate of increase in the retail price index, excluding mortgage payments (RPIX), was down to 2.4 per cent (''headline''

RPI was 2.3 per cent) and might have been even lower in the absence of higher indirect taxes. The strength of disinflation was remarkable, as the drop in sterling would "normally" have been expected to add about 2 percentage points to the annual rate of inflation. To some extent, such low inflation reflected the timing of favourable price influences (weak world commodity and oil prices and an "unanticipated" fall in total unit labour costs due to labour shakeout in late 1992, despite steadily rising output). These factors offset the initial boost to prices from sterling depreciation and the economy continued on a disinflationary track which proved far stronger than anticipated. The fundamental factor driving disinflation has been the large output gap, following the tightening of monetary policy in the early 1990s, in a context of balance sheet restructuring. The resulting disinflation was key in translating sterling's large nominal depreciation into a sustained improvement in international competitiveness, which helped the recovery. Microeconomic reforms pursued since the 1980s have also substantially changed attitudes concerning job security, work practices and pay, as well as competition and cost control, and these have been essential in the emergence of a more flexible and competitive economy.

A major unresolved issue is the extent to which the broadly observed increase in wage flexibility reflects a further fall in the "natural rate" of unemployment. Real wages rose surprisingly little in the second half of the 1980s despite the rapid fall in unemployment, and a range of empirical studies suggested a falling natural rate during this period. Real wages continued to increase between 1990 and 1992, when unemployment was rising, and while this was not too surprising given the degree of disinflationary pressure in goods markets, hysteresis effects may have interrupted the earlier fall in the natural rate. However, during 1993, wage moderation led to a fall in "underlying" inflation despite the currency depreciation and helped to "crowd-in" jobs – in stark contrast to the 1980s. This stabilisation of real wages relative to trend productivity may be indicative of a continuing decline in the natural rate of unemployment, although it is too early to draw firm conclusions. Moreover, greater real wage flexibility, as well as further improvements in training and education, may well be needed if unemployment (notably long-term) is to be lowered durably in the years ahead.

The pace of economic recovery picked up to an annual rate of close to 3 per cent in the last quarter of 1993. Output growth may slow temporarily in the face of higher tax burdens in the first half of 1994. But, given improved private sector balance sheet positions, rising employment, low inflation and a mild recovery in asset prices, output growth in the range of 2¾ to 3¼ per cent is projected in the coming two years. Business investment, which has so far been weak, typically picks up at this stage of the cycle, and investment intentions are responding to higher capacity utilisation and improved cash-flow. Higher business investment, a continuing recovery in the housing market and a swing in the stock cycle should all help to offset slower growth in private and public consumption in 1994 and beyond. The current account deficit is expected to remain close to 2 per cent of GDP, albeit widening somewhat. Inflation is expected to remain subdued, close to or slightly above the mid-point of the government's inflation target range. The main uncertainty surrounding this outlook is the degree of spare capacity in the economy and its implications for inflation as the economy recovers.

Since September 1992, the authorities have successfully established a new monetary policy framework to replace the ERM's previous role as a nominal anchor. Monetary policy is still the responsibility of the Chancellor of the Exchequer and is executed by the Bank of England. The new framework is based on targeting underlying inflation (RPIX) and increasing the transparency of policy decisions. The Government's target is to keep underlying inflation in a range of 1 to 4 per cent and to bring it down to the lower half of this range by the end of the present Parliament (no later than April 1997). Monetary policy decisions are based on an assessment of the inflation outlook, which takes account of a range of real and monetary indicators. Over the last eighteen months the Government has taken a number of steps to increase transparency. The recent decision to publish the minutes of the Chancellor's monthly meeting with the Governor of the Bank of England is a significant step forward.

Long-term bond yields started to rise sharply from February after the latest ¼ percentage point cut in UK base rates to 5¼ per cent. While higher bond yields were observed in many countries, UK rates rose by rather more than in Germany and the United States, although the differential remains low by recent historical standards. Inflation expectations in financial markets also appear to have risen, suggesting that the new monetary policy framework has not yet gained full credibility, even though inflation has been brought down to the middle of the Government's target range.

Current institutional arrangements should contribute to locking in low inflation, and over time the credibility of policy is likely to be improved by the moves towards greater transparency. But, the UK authorities need to remain vigilant to the emergence of future inflationary pressure. The acid test will only come as the economy approaches trend output, when pre-emptive action will be required to sustain low inflation.

The need to shift the balance of monetary and fiscal policies became a high priority following the sharp easing in monetary policy in September 1992. In view of the hesitant nature of the recovery, fiscal consolidation was backloaded. The March 1993 budget increased taxes mainly on households, starting in April 1994, by £6.7 and £10.3 billion in FY 1994/95 and FY 1995/96, respectively. The public sector borrowing requirement (PSBR) was forecast to increase to £50.1 billion (£55.6 billion excluding privatisation receipts) in FY 1993/94, almost 8 per cent of GDP, compared with £36.7 billion in FY 1992/93. Although the PSBR was projected to fall steadily in the medium-term, the debt to GDP ratio was then still projected to rise until FY 1996/97.

With indications of sustained recovery becoming clearer, fiscal consolidation was stepped up in the November budget. The new control total (essentially non-cyclical expenditure excluding debt interest) was cut by £3.6 billion in FY 1994/95 and £1.5 billion in FY 1995/96, implying a real expenditure decline in the current fiscal year and a small rise next year. Major savings included a "freeze" on government running costs and public sector wage bills; tighter controls on invalidity benefit and savings on defence, housing and transport programmes. Unemployment benefit and income support will be replaced from April 1996 by a "job seekers allowance". Further tax increases mainly on households were also announced to raise £1.7 billion in 1994/95, £4.9 billion in 1995/96 and £6.1 billion in the following fiscal year.

The November 1993 measures are projected to reduce the PSBR from its FY 1993/94 outturn of £45.9 billion (around $7\frac{1}{4}$ per cent of GDP) to £21 billion ($2\frac{3}{4}$ per cent of GDP) in FY 1996/97, assuming average GDP growth of 3 per cent over the medium term. Gross public debt is projected to peak at 51 per cent of GDP in 1997 and to decline thereafter. Although medium-term projections are sensitive to alternative growth outcomes, lower output growth by 0.5 per cent or so a year would not seriously jeopardize medium-term debt stabilisation. This process is also being supported by fundamental expenditure reviews, the first results being the social security measures announced in the November budget.

Together, the two 1993 budgets represent the sharpest fiscal adjustment since the early 1980s and should ensure sound medium-term public finances. The large increases in taxation scheduled from Spring 1994 onwards are likely to be absorbed by lower savings, despite slow growth in disposable incomes. Indeed, fiscal adjustment is timely and should favour a more balanced economic recovery by "crowding in" private investment and exports.

The United Kingdom has implemented a substantial number of supply-side reforms to improve the flexibility of the economy since the 1980s, although the process is by no means finished. The United Kingdom now has one of the least regulated labour markets in the OECD. Recent reforms have aimed at encouraging greater labour market participation, job-search and improved basic education standards. But, as in other OECD countries, much remains to be done to reduce "poverty traps", notably for low-skilled unemployed with dependents and for those receiving housing benefit. The efficiency of core public sector activities and the tax system has been improved. The VAT base has been widened and the tax advantage of mortgage interest relief eroded. However, other measures have had more ambiguous effects, shifting more tax payers into higher marginal tax brackets and/or leaving breaks in marginal effective tax rates. On the other hand, regulatory control of the newly privatised firms has been streamlined. Privatisation, deregulation and efforts to strengthen competition policy are continuing. Private sector management and finance are being brought into areas traditionally regarded as the exclusive domain of the public sector through the private finance initiative. And the basic state pension system remains financially sound despite the challenge of an ageing population.

Reform of the UK National Health Service, implemented in 1991, is a bold attempt to introduce elements of competition into the centrally-financed health care system which has succeeded in delivering adequate services to all citizens at reasonable overall cost to the economy. Reaching any overall conclusion about the impact of the reforms on the Health Service is premature. The main elements, the separation of purchaser and provider, and the creation of hospital Trusts and fundholding General Practitioners (GPs), are taking effect only gradually. The contracting capacity and the information to do it well are being acquired only slowly. There are costs to contracting and to monitoring. There has been little systematic research on the impact of the changes, something to which the Government had paid little attention until very recently. What research there is gives increasingly encouraging results. Fundholders and hospital Trusts appear to be contracting mainly with the same providers as before rather than effecting major changes in supply arrangements. Nevertheless, in a market as large and complex as that of health services, structural changes may realistically be expected to occur first only at the margins of traditional arrangements, and such changes do indeed appear to be happening. For example, the competitive element introduced, especially by fundholders, does appear to be making hospitals to respond to patients' needs and to improve efficiency. There are also indications that needs-based purchasing, rather than block contracts, is providing a clearer role for purchasing agencies. How to divide the purchasing functions between fundholding GPs and District Health Authorities, and how to link these to general goals for health outcomes are issues which are now being addressed in a variety of ways. Similarly the regulatory framework within which this "market" will develop has yet to be spelled out clearly, particularly as regards to exit, entry and structural adjustment in the hospital sector. But, these issues are under active consideration.

A key to success in transforming a command-and-control system into a more flexible and efficient one is to give competitive forces the chance and time to work themselves out fully before intervening to deal with any apparent market failures to produce desirable outcomes. The criticism that improved quality of services provided through GP fundholders is creating a two-tier system is a case in point. There has always been an element of inequity because the competence of GPs as well as the circumstances in which they practise differ substantially. There is no firm evidence that inequity has risen with the emergence of GP fundholders. If there were to be any transitory rise in inequity of this kind, it should be tolerated, as it would largely reflect efficiency gains. The answer should be sought by "levelling-up" – by expanding the number of fundholding GPs – rather than regulating them. Another case is closure of hospitals in large cities, which are experiencing financial difficulties because they are losing patients as a result of reforms. While it is understandable that political solutions are being sought for such sensitive issues, it is important that solutions go in the direction of facilitating, rather than retarding, adjustment and that the ways in which the downsizing takes place be guided by market signals. More generally, it will be imperative that the hospital Trusts make use of their new freedoms to invest (including those offered by the private finance initiative) or divest, as well as exercising fully the freedom already given to them in terms of personnel policies and capital allocation. To be able to deliver better performance, Trusts need to respond to sharper incentives than hitherto.

In conclusion, the United Kingdom has made major strides in restructuring its economy, establishing a new monetary policy framework, and putting the public finances on a sound medium-term footing. The economy is now at a favourable stage of the business cycle and could be experiencing steady output growth above the growth of potential output in late 1995. Unemployment is likely to be falling though remaining unacceptably high, still above its "natural rate". The current account deficit should still be manageable, although rising. This broadly favourable macroeconomic outlook should provide an opportunity to follow through on fiscal consolidation, while leaving monetary policy vigilant against the emergence of future inflation pressures. In the medium term, continued upgrading of the skill level of the labour force and on-going microeconomic reform would help to improve further the United Kingdom's economic performance and living standards.

Notes

1. See King, M. (1993), p. 7.

2. The ratio of financial and tangible wealth to GDP increased by almost 10 per cent from early 1992 to mid-1993, largely reflecting the recovery in financial markets, but still remains some 10 to 12 per cent below their peak levels in late 1988. See Bank of England (1994*a*).

3. See Bank of England (1994*b*), p. 18.

4. More than 90 per cent of UK mortgages are at variable rates and households' mortgage debt is currently just under 60 per cent of GDP. In other G-7 countries, mortgages are typically at fixed rates and are a much smaller ratio of GDP. In the United States 74 per cent of mortgages are at fixed rates and the ratio to GDP was 45 per cent at end-1993. In Japan, most housing loans are linked to the long-term prime rate and represented around 25 per cent of GDP in 1989. In Germany most housing loans are at fixed rates for 5 to 10 years and their ratio to GDP was around 25 per cent in 1990. In France loans are largely at fixed rates, with mortgage debt representing 22 per cent of GDP in 1992. In Italy, around a half of mortgages are at variable rates, but mortgage debt was only 7 per cent of GDP in 1986. In Canada mortgages are at fixed rates for a term of one to five years. For further details, see Bank of England (1991).

5. From early 1990, private consumption dropped 3½ per cent over the following seven quarters (despite a small rise in disposable income) (*cf.* Diagram 5). Households felt obliged to save high and rising proportions of income in the face of falling asset prices, thereby accentuating the cycle. From early 1989 to late 1992, the Halifax Building Society house price index dropped by almost 15 per cent or some 40 per cent in real terms. According to the Family Expenditure Survey, between 1989 and 1991 real consumption of households with mortgages fell by about 2 per cent, while for those without mortgages, it rose by almost 4 per cent. Non-housing expenditure fell by over 4 per cent for the first group of households, as they adjusted expenditure patterns to meet higher debt service, while it rose by 1 per cent for the second group. See King, M. *op. cit.,* p. 9.

6. Since 1990, there has been a shift to fixed rate mortgages (for more than 1 year) and by the third quarter of 1993 variable rate mortgages had dropped to 40 per cent of new mortgages.

7. From 1979 to 1990 non-financial corporations' interest payments relative to income rose from 13 to 24 per cent, but were significantly lower than in other EU countries. (By contrast, personal sector interest payments rose from 4 to 10.9 per cent of income and were more than double those in other EU countries. High personal interest payments reflect the debt-financed

UK consumer boom.) These differences reflect the greater access to capital markets that large UK firms have compared with those on the Continent. See Bank of England (1994c).

8. Firms repaid £6 billion in bank loans in 1993 compared with net borrowing of about £24 billion a year between 1988-1990. At the same time net capital issues rose sharply to around £15 billion in 1993, from £8.3 billion in 1992. These trends are a major reason for the slow growth of M4 (see Chapter II).

9. These typically range between 5 to 7 per cent of GDP.

10. Reforms in the 1980s included more flexible hiring and firing rules, lower redundancy pay and an end to closed shops. Employers were also allowed to make individual contracts and to derecognise unions under certain conditions. By 1993 some 20 per cent of work places surveyed had derecognised unions. As regards the tax-transfer system, reforms have lowered marginal tax rates and non-wage labour costs for part-time and low paid workers – thereby encouraging hiring in these groups. For example, workers earning less than £56 a week are exempt from National Insurance and sickness contributions, as are all employees working less than 8 hours a week. Non-wage costs in the United Kingdom are thus the lowest among EU countries. Unemployment replacement rates are also low, although housing allowance raises replacement rates sharply for low paid couples with dependents. The government also provides in-work benefits (Family credits) to ensure that low paid workers do not face punitive effective marginal tax rates.

11. For example, the Burton retail group has recently adopted a deliberate strategy of substituting part-time (typically female) for full time jobs.

12. For example, counterfactual simulations on the NIESR model (which is typical of mainstream UK macroeconomic models) indicate that had sterling remained in the ERM output growth would have been some 1 to 1.5 per cent lower in calendar 1993, and inflation 2 per cent lower. The latter estimate would allow for a small response of wages to depreciation. See Barrell et al. (1993).

13. Wage settlements are currently averaging around 2½ per cent and underlying average earnings around 3½ per cent, picking-up slightly in early 1994. Unit labour costs barely rose economy-wide in 1993 and fell in manufacturing.

14. Labour shakeout in late 1992 and early 1993 (despite rising output) produced an "unanticipated" fall in total unit wage costs. At the same time, steep drops in mortgage rates brought the "headline RPI" down quickly to 30-year lows of around 1½ to 2 per cent, and public sector pay rises were restricted to 1.5 per cent (see Chapter II), further damping price expectations. In the event, an extraordinarily large number of wage contracs were frozen or deferred in the aftermath of sterling depreciation – and typically settled later at low rates.

15. While there is evidence that the "natural rate" fell in the late 1980s, there is no consensus concerning its level. Empirical estimates of the "natural rate" vary from 3 to 10 per cent. OECD estimates for the late 1980s placed the rate between 7 to 9 per cent although the rate may have fallen in the 1990s. See OECD Economic Survey of the United Kingdom, 1990/91.

16. Standard econometric tests for this hypothesis would be to isolate any structural break in nominal (or real) wage behaviour relative to labour slack over time. Expectations-augmented Philips-curve type wage equations tend to over-predict nominal wage increases in the late

1980s and early 1990s, but the residuals are not statistically significant. Other tests for structural breaks are equally inconclusive.

17. Available estimates of employees' price expectations derived from the Gallup survey indicate that employees' price expectations have been well above actual inflation since 1991. As a result, recent nominal wage settlements have yielded larger than expected real wage gains. If these estimates are reliable, they would be consistent with greater *ex ante* real wage flexibility since 1991.

18. Financial market liberalisation, labour and product market deregulation, fast growth of small business and self-employment, and privatisation have forced UK business to compete more effectively or face bankruptcy or take-over. This has limited the ability of firms to live in the cost-plus environment of the past and changed business attitudes towards pay negotiations, part-time work and cost control. For example, competitive pressures have led to a sharp decline in multi-employer collective agreements and an accelerated shift to performance related pay and plant or company level bargaining. See, "Trends in pay flexibility", *Employment Gazette,* September 1993, p. 405-428.

19. In the past, the retail food sector was protected by zoning rules and restricted shopping hours and enjoyed large profit margins. More recently, competition in this sector has intensified with the introduction of foreign entry and structural and technological change. Traditional stores have been forced to compete to hold market share. Market leaders have invested in superstores, offering a wide range of products in city centres. At the same time, new foreign competitors offering a limited range of high volume basic generic products with low mark ups have also entered the market. Their competitive cost edge has been further enhanced by introduction of computer-based stock control and check-outs and a massive shift to lower paid part-time workers. See Bank of England (1994b), p. 9. For a description of the UK distribution system, see OECD (1993).

20. In addition, a tightening of the pricing formulae for the newly privatised companies (gas, electricity, water and telecom) and changes in regulatory control will lead to the breaking-up of quasi monopolies (*e.g.* gas and electricity distribution) and greater contestability of markets. These measures should contribute to greater efficiency, technical change and further moderation of service price inflation.

21. With the benefit of hindsight, the peak of the boom was in early 1990 and the economy entered recession one quarter before ERM entry.

22. See Central Statistical Office (1992). Estimates of investment income may also be systematically understated as they are based on the stock of foreign assets and liabilities and on relevant interest rate and equity yields. In fact, a large part of UK invisible earnings are generated by turnover in the large international banking sector.

23. Fiscal years end 31 March.

24. This implied that, notwithstanding cyclical variation in the PSBR, the sum of PSBRs would either be zero over the cycle or, less restrictively, that it would be zero when the economy regained trend output.

25. As a consequence of this forecasting error, fiscal policy was even more counter-cyclical than had been intended.

26. The financial deficit is a national accounts concept and is measured on an accruals basis. The PSBR is a cash-based concept.

27. The former item was reflected in miscellaneous financial transactions and the latter item in accruals adjustments.

28. Advance Corporation Tax (ACT) is paid by companies on distributed earnings (*i.e.* dividends). Companies are able to offset ACT against corporate-profits tax and dividend recipients receive an income-tax credit for ACT. The reduction in ACT raises revenue for the Government because pension funds, which do not pay tax on their earnings, receive a smaller tax credit and individuals paying the higher marginal income tax rate pay more tax.

29. The NCT accounts for around 85 per cent of general government expenditure excluding privatisation proceeds.

30. Cyclical social security is defined as unemployment benefit and income support paid to people of working age. It is excluded from the NCT to ensure that in future periods of strong economic growth savings on cyclical social security are not considered to provide scope for higher spending.

31. These decisions were partly based on the first "fundamental expenditure reviews" (social security, health, education and the Home Office), which examine the sustainability of individual programmes. They also identify areas from which the State might withdraw and where better targeting would be appropriate. Spending by all departments is to be reviewed before the end of the current parliament.

32. Plans to maintain public- (as opposed to general-government-) sector net investment at $1\frac{1}{2}$ per cent of GDP suggest that the public sector capital stock which was 68 per cent of GDP in 1992, may eventually settle at 62 to 77 per cent of GDP, assuming trend GDP growth of 2 to $2\frac{1}{2}$ per cent per annum. This calculation is based on the following relation for the steady-state capital-output ratio:

$$K/GDP = (I/GDP)*(1 + g)/g$$

where:

K/GDP is the capital-output ratio;

I/GDP is the net (of depreciation) investment-output ratio;

g is the real GDP growth rate.

Most estimates place UK trend GDP growth rate at $2 - 2\frac{1}{2}$ per cent.

It should be noted that estimates of the capital stock are uncertain and can be affected by movements in asset prices. For instance, the fall in land prices contributed to a fall in the estimated ratio of the general government capital stock to GDP between 1989 and 1992 at a time when general government gross investment was actually rising.

33. For the period beyond the current (expenditure) Survey (*i.e.* after 1996/97), real growth in the NCT of 1 per cent per annum is assumed.

34. Public expenditure plans are based on the conventional assumption that unemployment remains flat over the next three years, close to the level in November 1993 (2.75 million in Great Britain).

35. See H.M. Treasury (1994).

36. Real defence expenditure has been falling by an average ½ per cent per annum since FY 1985/86.

37. The exceptions were the "defence" and the "trade, industry, energy and employment" grouping.

38. Community health services cover a range of health-related service of a non-acute nature such as home nursing and care for the frail elderly.

39. That is, deaths from all causes (except suicides) between ages 0 and 64, weighted in each case by the number of years until age 65 which would have been reached.

40. In the case of life expectancy at age 60 (which, compared with other health outcome indicators, has a relatively high correlation with health expenditure per capita in OECD countries), the United Kingdom does not appear to do as well. The United Kingdom is at over one standard error below its "predicted" level based on a simple cross-section regression between the life expectancy and health spending variables.

41. More generally, these comparisons of volume growth should be treated with care as health prices are partly derived from accounting procedures for the public services that differ between countries.

42. Many studies have found that differences in GDP (or Total Domestic Expenditure) per capita are the most significant "predictors" of inter-country differences in per capita health spending (e.g. Newhouse (1977), Gerdtham (1991)). The causal mechanisms, if any, behind this relationship are not clear, however, and care is therefore required in drawing conclusions or policy inferences from the relationship. In almost all cases, the level or resources to be devoted to health care stems from collective rather than individual decisions. GDP per capita may be a proxy for a variety of factors, related more or less to income and economic well-being (possibly including the size of public budgets), which influence these health spending decisions.

43. For example, capitation rather than fee for service payment arrangements for doctors and a significant share of public spending in total health care. See Gerdtham (1991) for further analysis.

44. As has been pointed out in previous reviews of the health care sector, expenditure or budgetary control is often a problem in both publicly-and privately-managed insurance schemes. The French health care system (OECD, 1994) relies heavily on a reimbursement plan run by public insurers with private fee-for-service delivery of ambulatory services. The United States' quite diverse health care system – featuring large numbers of public and private insurers who reimburse fee-for service providers – is also characterised by extremely rapid expenditure growth (OECD, 1992). Both reviews emphasise the need for an enforceable health budget constraint backed up by measures that allow purchasers of health services to contract for delivery of a prespecified bundle of services at a competitively-determined price.

45. See the OECD, *Annual Survey of Italy* (1992), page 73, and *Annual Survey of Greece* (1991-92), page 56. Both analyses point more or less explicitly to public health systems that cannot compete effectively with private health services even though the public health service charges close to zero prices.

46. In fact, incentives may have been perverse in some cases. Where consultants had private practices in addition to their positions in hospitals, there was a potential conflict of interest. The consultant could offer to serve a patient through his private practice after informing the patient that, in order to obtain the same service through the NHS, he would have to spend a considerable time on the waiting list in the public sector.

47. Fundholders are accountable to the NHS Management Executive through regional health authorities. These frequently delegate day-to-day management of fundholders to the Family Health Service Authorities (FHSAs) who also have responsibility for administering the family doctor services provided by all GPs.

48. These pressures are limited by a number of factors. First, there are few GP fundholders in some districts; in these districts, then, there is little alternative to DHA purchasing. Another factor that limits competition is the fact that one cannot go to one GP for primary health care and to another for secondary health care purchasing. The two services continue to be "bundled" together. This might weaken competitive pressure in purchasing, especially if switching GPs by patients is costly.

49. This means that there is little direct incentive for under-serving.

50. In some market segments – notably for the frail elderly – private health care provision is important.

51. The King's Fund financed several research projects designed to evaluate the changes. The research results are published in Robinson and LeGrand (1994).

52. The Health Care and Hospital Service activity indicator.

53. The National Health Management Executive is issuing a series of detailed and informative guides to health needs assessments on an area basis using the best epidemiological research and a complementary series of assessments of the cost-effectiveness of health service interventions. A UK Clearing House for Information on the Assessment of Health Outcomes has been set up at the Nuffield Institute in Leeds. This will be a resource centre for work on health outcomes research. Government has also set up a Standing Committee on Health Technology Assessment which is in the process of evaluating treatments, approaches and technical changes in health care.

54. Fifty per cent of admissions are nonetheless immediate.

55. The Patient's Charter – part of a wider strategy which builds on the Government's Citizen's Charter initiative to improve standards in the delivery of public services generally – was brought into effect on 1 April 1992. It sets out the public's right to NHS services and introduced three new rights addressing information, complaints handling, and waiting times for inpatient treatment. The Charter also introduced the concept of standard setting (at national and local level) as a means to improve the quality of service delivery. Further revision is due in the autumn and will include more new standards which will strengthen current guarantees/standards for inpatient and outpatient waiting times and include new standards for hospital catering and community nursing appointments.

56. This is the result of the government policy pursued since 1961 to build large district general hospitals to serve most of the needs of the district. District Health Authorities were set up to run them.

57. For two local case studies and a discussion of the issues, see Bartlett and Harrison, 1993; Appleby *et al.*, 1994). One evaluation of purchasing in the West Midlands concluded: "Evidence from our project over the last three years suggests that purchasers were still trying to get to grips with the basic information they required to assess health care needs and make rational decisions concerning the choice of provider – based on quantifiable measures of quality, reliable data on prices, and, importantly, local opinion. But in addition, purchasers are only just beginning to grapple with the underlying methodologies of priority setting, the construction of contracts and the information implications of monitoring contract performance" (Appleby *et al.*, 1994, pp. 51-2).

58. "Department of Health, Practice Budgets for General Medical Practitioners", Working Paper 3, HMSO, 1989.

59. In Oxfordshire, for example, the net cost of ingredients for fundholders in dispensing practices increased by 10 per cent, for non-dispensers by 13 per cent but for non-fundholders by nearly 19 per cent (Bradlow and Coulter, 1993).

60. Excess capacity is a particular problem in London and in other big cities, whose large teaching hospitals had previously attracted patients from all over the country. This was because their specialists had national or international reputations and because the treatment they offered was essentially free to the district from which the patient came (or, to be more accurate, the cross charging was so complex that it did not enter into the decision process). Under the reforms, districts must pay for any patients sent to such hospitals, often much more than would be the case if patients were treated in a local hospital. This is resulting in the loss of custom by long-established teaching hospitals. Faced with the possibility that several famous London teaching hospitals might close, the government quickly removed the issue from the market place and appointed a committee to consider the future of London hospitals and a series of specialty reviews.

61. There have been some changes in a few areas – for example in ambulance trusts where changes in wage scales have followed the move to trust status.

62. The White Paper embodies an illness-related approach to improving the health status of the population and sets targets for desired health outcomes. The targets are grouped in five "key areas" selected on the basis of three criteria:
    – that they represent significant burdens of ill-health and/or premature mortality for the population;
    – that they are areas in which effective interventions may be possible;
    – that monitoring the results and measuring outcomes achieved are possible.
    The initial key areas are coronary heart disease and stroke, cancers, mental illness, HIV/AIDS and sexual health, and accidents.

63. Under capitation, GPs could shift the cost of difficult cases by sending them to hospital specialists. Since they now have to purchase specialist services out of the fundholding budget there is a cost to this behaviour.

64. See "Population health outcome indicators for the NHS – a feasibility study" and "Population health outcome indicators for the NHS, 1993 – England – a consultation document", DOH, 1993.

65. Principally, income support (which is means tested) and unemployment benefit.

66. JSA will be administered by a single Department of State. At present, two departments administer unemployment compensation: the Employment Service administers unemployment benefit; the Department of Social Security administers income support.

67. See Prais, S.J. (1993).

68. Smithers, Alan (1993).

69. *The Times*, 15 December 1993.

70. *Financial* Times editorial, December 22, 1993.

71. Bennett, R.J. *et al.* (1994).

72. By Sir Ron Dearing.

73. *The Economist*, March 12-18, 1994, p. 28.

74. *Ibid.*

75. David Soskice, *Financial Times*, 6 January 1994.

76. Provided that the price elasticity of demand is greater than zero.

77. The National Insurance Fund receives NICs and pays various contributory benefits. These include: retirement pension; unemployment, incapacity and related benefits; widow's benefit and family benefits. By for the largest of these benefits are retirement pension and invalidity benefit, which in FY 1993/94 represented respectively 71 per cent and 18 per cent of the total expenditure met from the National Insurance Fund. Around 86 per cent of the contributory benefits paid by the Fund are unrelated to contributions.

78. Indeed, optimal tax theory suggests that VAT rates should be relatively high on goods and services such as domestic power and fuel for which the price elasticity of demand is comparatively low. Allowing for administrative costs, however, a single-rate VAT system with a minimum of exceptions is likely to be more efficient.

79. For a discussion of environmental issues see OECD (1993*b*).

80. Giles, Christopher and Paul Johnson (1994).

81. *Ibid.*, pp. 14-21.

82. *Financial Times*, 1 October 1993, editorial.

83. Next Steps agencies are executive agencies which have been created within government departments to carry out operational (as opposed to policy) functions. These agencies are given greater managerial autonomy than other parts of government departments to achieve clearly defined objectives within agreed resource constraints. As of April 1993, around 60 per cent of civil servants were working in Next Steps agencies or other organisations operating along similar lines.

84. Specifically, for a person to receive the full rate of basic pension, they must have made NICs during 90 per cent of the years between 16 and the pensionable age (*i.e.* 44.1 years for men and 39.6 years for women). This contributions test is eased in cases where an individual is prevented from working for reasons such as home care responsibilities. The pension is reduced on a pro-rata basis for those with contribution periods which are shorter but still greater than 10 years. Contribution periods below 10 years do not qualify for any basic-pension rights.

85. That is, those with earnings above the lower earning limit (LEL) who have not contracted out into an approved occupational or private pension scheme.

86. Relevant earnings are those on which contributions have been paid in any tax year, revalued in line with the general level of earnings up to the year before that in which pension age is attained. For those not contracted out of SERPs (into approved occupational or private pension schemes), contributions are paid in any tax year on earnings between the lower earning limit (LEL) and the upper earning limit (UEL).

87. This means that, ultimately, pension rights will accrue at 20/49 per cent. When set up in 1978, the scheme promised more generous benefits – 25 per cent of average earnings over the best 20 years. The Social Security Act 1986 provided for the eventual replacement of these benefits with those currently promised but provided transitional arrangements. The right to benefits accrued before 1988 was preserved. For those retiring before April 2000, there was effectively no change – they will receive a pension based on an accrual rate of 25/N per cent for all relevant earnings, where N is the number of tax years in the earner's working life from April 1978 to pension age, with a minimum value of 20. For those retiring between April 2000 and April 2009, there will be a phased reduction in the accrual rate from 25/N per cent to 20/N per cent. For later retirements, the accrual rate for post-1988 earnings will be the ultimate rate of 20/N per cent.

88. NICs are paid by employers, employees and the self-employed. There is an upper earnings limit (UEL) on employee and self-employed NICs but no UEL for employer contributions.

89. Dilnot, A. and P. Johnson (1992).

90. *Ibid.*

91. The State provides a small contribution to contracted out occupational pensions. To qualify for contracted-out status, schemes must provide at least the Guaranteed Minimum Pension (GMP), which is roughly equivalent to what a scheme member would have received had he or she remained in SERPS. The State tops-up the GMP where SERPS benefits are not matched exactly. For example, while SERPS offers full price indexation of pensions in payment, occupational schemes are only required to price protect the GMP to a maximum of 3 per cent.

92. The discussion in this paragraph is mostly based on A. Dilnot and P. Johnson, *ibid.*, p. 4.

93. Thus, contributions made at age 20 have the same value as those made at age 59, even though the former contributions would have earned 39 years of returns in a private scheme.

94. A key assumption in this regard is that the unemployment rate is 5 per cent. Were the unemployment rate to be 7 per cent, NICs would need to be 1.0-1.2 per cent higher over the first half of next century under price upratings. Under earnings upratings, the increases would be 1.5-1.8 per cent.

95. National Insurance Fund (1990).

96. *Ibid.*, pp. 29-30.

97. Real earnings are assumed to grow at an annual rate of $1\frac{1}{2}$ per cent.

References

ppleby, J., P. Smith, W. Ranade, V. Little and R. Robinson (1994), "Monitoring Managed Competition" in Robinson and LeGrand, (eds), "Revaluating the NHS Reforms", Kings Fund Institute, London.

udit Commission (1993), *Practices Make Perfect: the role of the Family Health Services Authority,* HMSO, London.

ınk of England (1991), "Housing Finance", *Bank of England Quarterly.*

ınk of England (1994*a*), *Bank of England Quarterly,* February, p. 50.

ank of England (1994*b*), *Inflation Report,* February.

ank of England (1994*c*), "Fixed and floating rate finance in the United Kingdom and abroad", *Bank of England Quarterly,* February, pp. 40–41.

ʃarr, N., H. Glennerster and J. Le Grand (1988), *Reform and the NHS,* Welfare State Paper No. 32, London School of Economics.

ʒarrell, R., A. Britton and N. Pain (1993), "When the time was right? The U.K. experience of the ERM", *National Institute of Economic and Social Research, Discussion Paper* No. 58, December.

Bartlett, W. and L. Harrison (1994), "Quasi Markets and the National Health Service Reforms" in Le Grand and Bartlett, "Quasi Markets and Social Policy", Macmillan, London.

Bennett, R.J. *et al.* (1994), "Local employment and business services: Britain's experience with TECs", London School of Economics.

Bloor, K. and A. Maynard (1993), *Expenditure on the NHS During and After the Thatcher Years: its Growth and Utilisation,* Discussion Paper 113, Centre for Health Economics, York.

Bradlow, J. and A. Coulter (1993), "Effect of fundholding and indicative prescribing schemes on general practitioners' prescribing costs", *British Medical Journal,* Vol. 307, pp. 1186-9.

Central Statistics Office (1992), *"Pink book 1992".*

Dilnot, A. and P. Johnson (1992), "What Pension Should the State Provide", *Fiscal Studies,* Vol. 13, No. 4.

Enthoven, A. (1985), *Reflections on the Management of the NHS,* Nuffield Trust, London.

Gerdtham, Ulf-G. (1991), *Essays on international comparisons of Health Care Expenditure,* Linköping Studies in Art and Science 66, Linköping.

Giles, Christopher and Paul Johnson (1994), ''Taxes up, taxes down: the effects of a decade of tax changes'', Institute for Fiscal Studies Commentary, No. 41.

Glennerster, H., M. Matsaganis and P. Owens (1992), *A Foothold for Fundholding,* Kings Fund Institute, London.

Glennerster, H. *et al.* (1994), ''Wild Card or Winning Hand: GP fundholding'' in Robinson and LeGrand, *op. cit.*

Gudex, C., A. Williams, Jourdan *et al.* (1990), ''Prioritising Waiting Lists'', *Health Trends,* Vol. 2, No. 3, pp. 103-8.

H.M. Treasury (1993), *Financial Statement and Budget Report 1994-5,* HMSO, London.

H.M. Treasury (1994), *Forecasts for the UK economy – A comparison of independent forecasts,* London.

Jones, D., C. Lester and R. West (1994), ''Monitoring Changes in Health Services for Older People'' in Robinson and LeGrand, *op. cit.*

Jowell, R. *et al.* (1991), *British Social Attitudes 8th Report,* Gower, Aldershot.

Kerrison, S., T. Packwood and M. Buxton (1994), ''Monitoring Medical Audit'' in Robinson and LeGrand, *op. cit.*

King, M. (1993), ''Debt deflation: theory and evidence'', *Discussion Paper* No. 175, London School of Economics, November.

Kings Fund Institute (1988), *Health Finance: Assessing the Options,* Kings Fund, London.

Klein, R. (1991), ''Making sense of inequalities: a response to Peter Townsend'', *International Journal of Health Services,* Vol. 21, pp. 175-81.

Klein, R. and S. Redmayne (1992), *Patterns of Priorities: a study of the purchasing and rationing policies of health authorities,* NAHAT, Birmingham.

LeGrand *et al.* (1991), ''Quasi Markets and Social Policy'', *Economic Journal,* Vol. 101, pp. 1256-88.

LeGrand, J. and W. Bartlett (1993), *Quasi- Markets and Social Policy,* MacMillan, London.

LeGrand J. and W. Bartlett, ''The Performance of Trusts'' in Robinson and LeGrand, *op. cit.*

LeGrand, J. and R. Illsley (1991), ''Regional Inequalities in Mortality'', LSE Welfare State Discussion Paper, LSE London and forthcoming.

LeGrand, J., D. Winter and Woolley (1990), ''NHS Safe in Whose Hands?'' in *The State of Welfare* ed., J. Hills, Oxford University Press, Oxford.

Mahon, A., D. Wilkin and C. Whitehouse (1994), ''Choice of Hospital for Elective Surgery Referral: GPs and Patients' Views'' in Robinson and LeGrand, *op. cit.*

Maxwell, M., D. Heaney, J.G.R. Howie and S. Noble (1993), ''General practice fundholding: observations on prescribing patterns and costs using the defined daily dose method'', *British Medical Journal,* Vol. 307, pp. 1190-94.

Maynard, A. (1993), ''Competition in the U.K. National Health Service: Mission impossible'', *Health Policy,* Vol. 23, pp. 193-204.

National Health Service Management Plan (1993), *The National Health Service Management Executive Business Plan 1993/4,* HMSO, London.

National Insurance Fund (1990), *Long-term financial estimates.*

Newhouse, J.P. (1977), "Medical care expenditure: a cross national survey", *Journal of Human Resources,* 12, pp. 115-125.

OECD (1987), *Financing and Delivering Health Care,* OECD, Paris.

OECD (1991), *Market Type Mechanisms,* OECD, Paris.

OECD (1992), *The Reform of Health Care: a Comparative Analysis of Seven Countries,* OECD, Paris.

OECD (1993a), "The Distribution Sector in the United Kingdom", *OECD Economics Department Working Papers* No. 140.

OECD (1993b), *Economic Survey of the United Kingdom,* January.

Prais, S.J. (1993), *Economic Performance and Education: the nature of Britain's deficiencies,* National Institute of Economic and Social Research, Discussion Paper No. 52.

Propper, C. and A. Maynard (1990), "Whither the Private Health Care Sector" in A.J. Culyer, A.K. Maynard, and J.W. Posnett, *Competition in Health Care: Reforming the NHS,* Macmillan, London.

Propper, C. and O'Donnell (1991), "Equity and the Distribution of NHS Resources", *Journal of Health Economics,* Vol. 10, pp. 1-19.

Propper, C. (1993), "Quasi-Markets, Contracts and Quality in Health and Social Care: The US Experience" in LeGrand and Bartlett, *op. cit.*

Robinson, R. and J. LeGrand (eds), (1994), *Evaluating the NHS Reforms,* Kings Fund Institute, London.

Saltman, R.B. and C. von Otter (1992), *Planned Markets and Public Competition,* Open University Press, Milton Keynes.

Smithers, Alan (1993), All Our Futures – Britain's Educational Revolution.

Social and Community Planning Research (1994), forthcoming.

Taylor-Gooby, P. (1991), "Attachment to the Welfare State" in Jowell, *op. cit.*

Townsend, P. (1990), "Widening Inequalities in Health: a rejoinder to Rudolf Klein", *International Journal of Health Services,* Vol. 20, pp. 363-72.

U.K. DoH (1989), *Working for Patients,* Cm 555, HMSO, London.

U.K. DoH (1991a), *Research and Development Strategy,* HMSO, London.

U.K. DoH (1991b), *The Patients' Charter,* HMSO, London.

U.K. DoH (1992), *The Health of the Nation,* Cm 1986, HMSO, London.

U.K. DoH (1993), *The Government's Expenditure Plans 1993-94 to 1995-96: Departmental Report,* Cm 2212, HMSO, London.

Whitehead M. (1992), *The Health Divide in Inequalities in Health,* Penguin, Harmondworth.

Annex

Calendar of main economic events

1992

July

The Government announces a new medium-term control framework for public expenditure. The global public limit set by the Public Expenditure Cabinet is to be considered binding, with bilateral discussions between Treasury and spending departments only to concern the allocation of these resources, rather than the total. The public expenditure limit for FY 1993/94 is held at £245.5 billion and growth in non-cyclical and non-interest expenditure is to be restricted to 3 per cent and 3.25 per cent respectively in 1994/95 and 1995/96.

September

A run on sterling develops in the run-up to the French referendum on the Maastricht Treaty. The base lending-rate is increased by 2 per cent to 12 per cent on the morning of 16 September. A further increase in the base rate to 15 per cent is announced on the same day. These increases fail to stem selling pressure on sterling and its participation in the ERM is suspended later that day. Base rates are restored to 10 per cent the following morning.

The base rate is cut by 1 per cent to 9 per cent.

October

The Chancellor of the Exchequer announces a framework for conducting monetary policy outside the ERM. Monetary policy is to target a short-run underlying inflation rate (RPI excluding mortgage rates) of 1 to 4 per cent, with an ultimate objective of attaining price stability, defined as inflation less than 2 per cent. Monetary conditions are to be assessed with reference to a wide range of indicators. The Chancellor also announces that the government intends to rejoin the ERM when conditions are appropriate but that this is unlikely to be soon.

Plans to close a substantial proportion of coal mines are announced, but the timing and magnitude of these closures are subsequently subject to review.

The base rate is cut by 1 per cent to 8 per cent.

November

The November 1992 Autumn Statement contained medium-term public expenditure plans and a number of measures to assist recovery. Measures included:

- first-year capital allowances for investment were temporarily increased for the next year from 25 per cent to 40 per cent;
- the remaining 5 per cent car tax was abolished;
- local authorities will be allowed to spend receipts from council house sales between now and the end of next year on capital projects (estimated at £1.75 billion);
- housing associations will spend £750 million by the end of this financial year to buy repossessed empty houses, while increasing the stock of subsidised houses available to low income families;
- provision of an additional £700 million of export credit cover;
- measures were announced to encourage private-sector participation in public sector infrastructure projects as well as to enhance the use of leasing arrangements by public companies.

The new planning total for general government expenditure in FY 1993/94 was held at £244.5 billion, with savings from limiting public sector pay increases to 1.5 per cent over the coming year and reductions in such areas as defence, offsetting increases elsewhere (health, education, social security and training programmes). The PSBR is now forecast at £37 billion, $6\frac{1}{4}$ per cent of GDP in FY 1992/93, up from the £28 billion in the March 1992 Budget. (Excluding privatisation proceeds the PSBR is projected at £45 billion, $7\frac{1}{2}$ per cent of GDP).

The new planning totals announced for 1994/95 and 1995/96 of £253.6 and £263.3 billion respectively would imply real growth in government expenditure of 0.7 per cent in 1994/95 and 1.0 per cent in 1995/96 following 2.3 per cent real growth in 1993/94, given the government's inflation assumptions of around 3 per cent for the GDP deflator over this period.

The base lending rate was lowered to 7 per cent accompanying the Autumn Statement.

1993

January

The base rate is cut to 6 per cent.

February

Wide range of public spending reviews launched to question the basic principles of the welfare state.

March

PSBR forecast to reach £50 billion in 1993/94. Tax measures include VAT on domestic fuel, mortgage relief to be restricted to 20 per cent from April 1994. Most excise duties raised by 5 per cent.

May

Kenneth Clarke replaces Normant Lamont as Chancellor of the Exchequer.

June

U.K. cabinet sets toughest public spending limits in 15 years.

August

All ERM currencies except guilder and deutschemark to have wider bands of 15 per cent, following exchange market turmoil.

November

The base rate is cut to $5^{1}/_{2}$ per cent in advance of the budget.

The first unified budget reduces mortgage interest relief to 15 per cent by 1995/96. Tax allowances are frozen. A freeze on public sector running costs was introduced until 1997 as part of a cut in public spending. Student grants are cut by 10 per cent. PSBR to be brought to zero in the medium-term.

1994

February

The Bank of England reduces base rates by 0.25 percentage points to 5.25 per cent.

April

FY 1993/94 PSBR outturn of £45.9 billion, $7^{1}/_{4}$ per cent of GDP is announced.

STATISTICAL AND STRUCTURAL ANNEX

Table A. Expenditure on GDP
£ million

	GDP at factor cost (expenditure-based)	Total expenditure at market prices	Total domestic demand	Consumers' expenditure	Public current expenditure	Fixed investment	Change in stocks	Exports of goods and services	Imports of goods and services	Indirect taxes less subsidies
At current prices										
1984	280 653	418 130	326 498	198 820	71 201	55 181	1 296	91 632	92 763	44 714
1985	307 902	456 332	354 291	217 485	75 267	60 718	821	102 041	98 988	49 442
1986	328 272	486 064	388 179	241 554	80 911	65 032	682	97 885	101 221	56 571
1987	360 675	535 118	428 721	265 290	87 045	75 052	1 334	106 397	111 737	62 706
1988	401 428	596 226	488 953	299 449	93 641	91 118	4 745	107 273	124 796	70 002
1989	441 759	658 765	537 279	327 363	101 796	104 535	3 585	121 486	142 808	74 198
1990	478 886	699 403	566 119	347 527	112 934	106 776	-1 118	133 284	148 285	72 232
1991	494 824	714 875	580 727	365 057	124 205	96 534	-5 069	134 148	140 775	79 276
1992	514 498	745 665	605 414	382 362	132 657	92 387	-1 992	140 251	149 455	81 712
1993	543 751	794 196	636 152	405 647	136 895	93 235	375	158 044	166 322	84 123
At 1990 prices										
1984	392 067	554 716	451 697	266 486	105 177	78 270	1 764	103 019	103 283	59 366
1985	407 844	573 913	464 750	276 742	105 267	81 575	1 336	109 163	105 957	60 112
1986	424 214	601 377	487 330	295 622	106 824	83 685	1 199	114 047	113 255	63 908
1987	443 817	633 690	513 083	311 234	107 858	92 260	1 731	120 607	122 075	67 798
1988	465 746	674 658	553 461	334 591	108 612	104 726	5 532	121 197	137 443	71 469
1989	476 226	696 553	569 717	345 406	110 139	110 503	3 669	126 836	147 615	72 712
1990	478 886	699 403	566 119	347 527	112 934	106 776	-1 118	133 284	148 285	72 232
1991	467 720	679 447	547 333	339 993	115 797	96 265	-4 722	132 114	140 248	71 479
1992	465 404	685 550	549 447	339 902	116 604	94 714	-1 773	136 103	149 056	71 090
1993	474 374	700 667	560 300	348 315	116 071	95 452	462	140 367	154 206	72 158
Seasonally adjusted										
1993 1	117 546	173 392	138 263	86 019	28 892	24 009	-657	35 129	38 032	17 814
2	118 016	174 099	139 357	86 447	29 064	23 457	389	34 742	37 915	18 168
3	118 976	175 625	140 029	87 453	29 115	23 699	-238	35 596	38 564	18 085
4	119 836	177 551	142 651	88 396	29 000	24 287	968	34 900	39 695	18 091

Source: Central Statistical Office, *Economic Trends.*

Table B. Gross domestic fixed capital formation
£ million

	Total	Private sector[1]	General government[1]	Public corporations[1]	Vehicles, ships and aircraft	Plant and machinery	Dwellings Private	Dwellings Public	Other new building and works[2]	Energy and water supply	Manufacturing
At current prices											
1984	55 181	41 021	6 719	7 441	5 664	20 266	9 186	2 746	17 319	2 779	8 380
1985	60 718	47 915	6 872	5 931	6 439	23 870	9 683	2 536	18 190	2 660	10 283
1986	65 032	52 002	7 509	5 521	6 222	24 690	11 526	2 614	19 980	2 792	10 105
1987	75 052	62 914	7 577	4 561	7 805	27 073	13 333	2 916	23 925	2 798	11 040
1988	91 118	80 032	6 506	4 580	8 849	31 504	17 601	2 914	30 250	3 119	12 415
1989	104 535	89 486	9 582	5 467	10 324	36 382	18 234	3 846	35 749	3 943	14 248
1990	106 776	89 162	12 659	4 955	10 266	36 762	16 530	4 227	38 991	4 742	14 227
1991	96 534	80 612	12 143	3 779	8 646	34 678	14 467	2 820	35 923	5 608	13 183
1992	92 387	75 563	12 569	4 255	8 450	34 037	15 152	2 554	32 194	6 349	12 485
1993	93 235	77 313	11 354	4 568	9 601	35 875	15 005	2 664	30 090	6 094	12 810
At 1990 prices											
1984	78 270	59 953	8 405	9 537	8 982	24 083	15 310	3 887	26 437	3 638	10 975
1985	81 575	65 820	8 441	7 277	9 480	27 081	14 899	3 489	26 486	3 334	12 710
1986	83 685	67 877	9 163	6 645	8 493	27 512	16 681	3 489	27 510	3 404	12 097
1987	92 260	78 013	9 027	5 220	9 846	29 086	17 957	3 771	31 600	3 304	12 641
1988	104 726	92 043	7 579	5 104	10 372	33 770	21 303	3 506	35 775	3 490	13 846
1989	110 503	94 778	10 054	5 671	11 231	37 925	19 686	4 136	37 525	4 094	14 984
1990	106 776	89 162	12 659	4 955	10 266	36 762	16 530	4 227	38 991	4 742	14 227
1991	96 265	79 697	12 688	3 880	8 008	33 957	13 942	2 836	37 522	5 619	12 803
1992	94 714	76 530	13 760	4 424	7 322	32 895	14 671	2 724	37 102	6 520	11 907
1993	95 452	76 976	13 504	4 972	8 213	33 247	14 524	2 967	36 501	6 281	11 813
Seasonally adjusted											
1993 1	24 009	18 480	4 104	1 425	2 156	8 193	3 551	797	9 312	1 475	2 977
2	23 457	19 000	3 347	1 110	1 846	8 197	3 706	676	9 032	1 628	2 905
3	23 699	19 170	3 364	1 165	2 166	8 347	3 578	754	8 854	1 624	2 968
4	24 287	20 326	2 689	1 272	2 045	8 510	3 689	740	9 303	1 554	2 963

1. Including purchases less sales of land and existing buildings.
2. Including transfer costs of land and buildings.
Source: Central Statistical Office, Economic Trends.

Table C. Household appropriation account

£ billion

	Compensation of employees	Property and income	Transfers received	Gross total income	Direct taxes	Social security contributions	Other current deductions[1]	Disposable income	Private consumption	Personal savings ratio[2]	Real income[3]
1984	181.4	59.2	41.6	282.2	34.7	22.3	1.5	223.6	198.8	11.1	3.6
1985	196.9	64.9	45.4	307.1	37.8	24.2	1.7	243.5	217.5	10.7	3.4
1986	212.4	71.6	49.5	333.4	40.8	26.2	1.9	264.5	241.6	8.7	4.5
1987	229.8	79.0	50.8	359.7	43.5	28.6	2.1	285.4	265.3	7.1	3.4
1988	255.6	92.6	52.2	400.4	48.3	32.1	2.3	317.7	299.4	5.7	6.0
1989	283.5	104.9	54.0	442.4	53.6	32.9	3.0	352.9	327.4	7.2	4.9
1990	312.4	116.1	58.9	487.4	61.5	34.7	11.2	380.1	347.5	8.6	2.1
1991	328.3	119.1	69.2	516.6	63.3	36.4	10.8	406.1	365.1	10.1	-0.5
1992	341.3	128.1	79.5	548.9	64.9	37.3	10.7	436.1	382.4	12.3	2.5
1993	350.5	133.7	87.8	572.0	64.2	38.6	10.9	458.4	405.6	11.5	1.5
Seasonally adjusted											
1993 1	86.7	33.2	21.7	141.6	16.0	9.6	2.8	113.3	99.1	12.6	3.2
2	87.1	33.7	21.9	142.6	16.1	9.5	2.7	114.4	100.4	12.2	1.6
3	88.0	33.4	22.0	143.3	16.0	9.7	2.7	114.9	102.2	11.0	0.7
4	88.7	33.5	22.2	144.4	16.1	9.8	2.8	115.7	104.0	10.2	0.6

1. This series includes other current transfers and from 2nd quarter 1989, payments of the community charge.
2. As a percentage of disposable income.
3. Percentage change.

Source: Central Statistical Office, Economic Trends.

Table D. **Consumption and investment**

Seasonally adjusted

	Consumer demand				Investment					
	Retail sales		New registrations	Changes in hire purchase debt total	Capital expenditure of		Engineering new domestic orders [1]	Housing starts		Investment in stocks (manufacturing)
	Total	Non-food			Manufacturing industry	Other industries		Private	Public	
	Volume 1990 = 100		Thousand, monthly averages	£ million, end of period	£ million, at 1990 prices		Average monthly sales 1990 = 100	Thousand		£ million at 1990 prices
1984	79.2	74.1	147	1 551	10 975	33 859	70	158.3	40.0	1 131
1985	82.8	78.2	154	2 309	12 710	36 361	67	165.7	34.5	-612
1986	87.2	83.7	157	2 385	12 097	37 904	69	180.1	33.5	-686
1987	91.6	89.4	168	3 498	12 641	44 692	76	196.8	32.8	-486
1988	97.3	96.9	184	3 639	13 846	51 981	102	221.4	30.9	992
1989	99.2	99.3	192	3 248	14 984	58 632	107	170.0	31.1	200
1990	100.0	100.0	167	3 531	14 227	58 095	100	135.4	27.1	-1 914
1991	98.8	96.9	133	1 043	12 803	50 842	88	135.0	26.5	-3 564
1992	99.6	96.2	133	358	11 907	48 848	89	120.1	36.4	-2 171
1993	103.0	99.3	148	2 939	11 813	50 289	90	142.3	43.3	-1 024
1993 1	101.8	98.3	142	446	2 977	12 701	89	34.0	13.1	-741
2	102.4	99.0	145	547	2 905	12 039	89	35.0	10.6	266
3	103.4	99.9	150	900	2 968	12 476	90	35.7	9.7	-590
4	104.3	99.9	157	1 046	2 963	13 073	92	37.6	9.9	41

1. Received by mechanical, instrument and electrical engineering, excluding transport equipment.
Source: Central Statistical Office, *Economic Trends* and *Monthly Digest of Statistics.*

127

Table E. Production and manpower

Seasonally adjusted

	GDP at factor cost	GDP per person employed[1]	Industrial production	Manufacturing production	Unemployed[2]	Unfilled vacancies (adults)	Employment		Hours of overtime worked in manufacturing industries
							Total	Manufacturing industries	
	1990 = 100				Thousand		1990 = 100		Million per week
1984	81.9	90.5	87.7	82.2	2 998	150	90.4	104.2	11.39
1985	85.2	92.7	88.0	84.5	3 113	162	91.3	103.6	11.98
1986	88.6	96.3	90.1	85.6	3 180	189	92.0	101.3	11.72
1987	92.7	98.9	93.7	89.6	2 822	235	93.8	100.5	12.63
1988	97.3	100.4	98.2	95.9	2 294	249	96.9	101.8	13.42
1989	99.4	100.1	100.3	100.2	1 784	220	99.3	102.2	13.44
1990	100.0	100.0	100.0	100.0	1 662	174	100.0	100.0	12.44
1991	97.7	100.4	96.1	94.7	2 287	118	97.3	93.5	9.63
1992	97.1	102.5	95.6	93.9	2 765	117	94.8	88.9	9.46
1993	99.0	105.8	98.1	95.5	2 901	128	93.7	86.7	9.09
1993 1	98.2	105.1	96.7	95.2	2 952	121	93.5	86.7	9.14
2	98.6	105.5	97.5	95.6	2 926	123	93.5	86.6	8.80
3	99.4	106.0	98.6	95.5	2 914	128	93.8	86.8	9.37
4	100.0	106.5	99.6	95.7	2 812	139	93.9	86.7	9.10

1. Based on output-based GDP.
2. Claimants aged 18 and over.
Source: Central Statistical Office, Economic Trends, and Department of Employment, Employment Gazette.

Table F. Wages, prices and external position

Seasonally adjusted

	Average earnings [1]	Producer prices manufacturing, home market*	Retail prices*	Unit values*		Exports (fob)	Imports (fob)	Visible trade	Current balance
				Exports	Imports				
	1990 = 100			1990 = 100		£ million			
1984	60.9	75.4	70.7	93.1	91.8	70 265	75 601	-5 336	1 482
1985	66.1	79.4	75.0	98.1	96.3	77 991	81 336	-3 345	2 238
1986	71.3	83.8	77.6	88.4	91.8	72 627	82 186	-9 559	-871
1987	76.8	86.7	80.8	91.5	94.6	79 153	90 735	-11 582	-4 983
1988	83.5	89.8	84.7	92.4	93.7	80 346	101 826	-21 480	-16 617
1989	91.1	94.1	91.3	96.6	97.7	92 154	116 837	-24 683	-22 512
1990	100.0	100.0	100.0	100.0	100.0	101 718	120 527	-18 809	-18 268
1991	108.0	105.4	105.9	101.4	101.2	103 413	113 697	-10 284	-7 652
1992	114.6	108.7	109.8	103.5	102.1	107 047	120 453	-13 406	-9 967
1993	118.5	113.0	111.5	113.5	109.5	120 839	134 519	-13 680	-10 927
1993 1	118.0	111.2	109.9	113.0	110.7	29 893	33 488	-3 595	-3 378
2	117.9	113.1	111.7	111.6	109.6	29 660	32 990	-3 330	-3 296
3	118.7	113.5	112.0	113.8	109.7	30 629	33 805	-3 176	-1 916
4	119.6	113.9	112.4	115.5	108.1	30 657	34 236	-3 579	-2 337

* Not seasonally adjusted.
1. From 1988 onwards, data are 1990 = 100; the pre-1988 data have been estimated from previous 1985 = 100 figures.
Source: Central Statistical Office, Economic Trends, and Department of Employment, Employment Gazette.

Table G. **Net capital transactions**

Not seasonally adjusted, £ million

	Current balance	UK investment overseas			Lending overseas by		Other external government transactions	Total investment and other capital transactions	Drawings on (+) or additions to (−) reserves	Balancing item
		Total	Direct	Portfolio	UK banks	UK residents other than banks and general government				
1984	1 798	−14 682	−6 217	−8 465	9 780	−3 637	−784	−9 322	908	6 616
1985	2 790	−10 924	−3 943	−6 981	7 018	2 637	−706	−1 975	−1 758	943
1986	−871	−16 273	−5 812	−10 461	13 154	3 168	−332	−283	−2 891	4 044
1987	−4 983	17 953	−9 698	27 651	1 758	−1 708	1 034	19 037	−12 012	−2 043
1988	−16 617	−3 549	−8 857	5 308	14 397	2 321	−55	13 114	−2 761	6 265
1989	−22 512	−23 198	−2 936	−20 262	16 243	18 981	1 949	13 975	5 440	3 097
1990	−18 268	−770	7 976	−8 746	6 338	5 795	−326	11 037	−76	7 308
1991	−7 652	−9 819	191	−10 010	8 029	14 420	−3 223	9 407	−2 679	924
1992	−9 967	−14 054	−1 056	−12 998	−1 645	22 504	−1 946	4 859	1 407	3 704
1993	−10 927	−61 895	−7 248	−54 647	27 299	47 947	−3 750	9 601	−701	2 027
1993 1	−3 444	−26 946	−1 630	−25 316	16 978	13 056	−3 023	65	463	2 916
2	−3 884	4 888	−891	5 779	−4 774	1 669	17	1 800	−750	2 834
3	−2 735	−5 333	−1 479	−3 854	3 254	7 605	−31	5 495	−540	−2 220
4	−864	−34 504	−3 248	−31 256	11 841	25 617	−713	2 241	126	−1 503

Source: Central Statistical Office, *Financial Statistics.*

Table H. **Foreign assets and liabilities**

End of period

	Effective exchange rate	Official reserves		Sterling balances[1]		Outstanding official borrowing from abroad[2]
		Total	of which: Convertible currencies	Official	Other holders	
	1985 = 100	$ million		£ million		$ million
1984	100.5	15 694	7 577	7 755	26 825	11 283
1985	100.0	15 543	8 486	9 327	31 236	14 637
1986	91.5	21 923	13 781	9 585	37 160	19 325
1987	90.1	44 326	35 726	13 947	44 766	19 069
1988	95.5	51 685	42 184	15 953	56 948	15 751
1989	92.6	38 645	30 453	16 229	68 678	14 035
1990	91.3	38 464	30 553	18 895	83 238	14 699
1991	91.7	44 126	36 122	16 734	75 385	17 191
1992	88.4	41 654	34 338	16 349	79 368	32 982
1993	80.2	42 926	36 210	25 801	75 970	29 291
1993 1	78.5	40 898	33 870	18 312	79 414	29 945
2	80.2	41 897	35 096	19 606	76 948	29 737
3	81.0	43 044	36 182	23 008	75 344	30 629
4	81.0	42 926	36 210	25 801	75 970	29 291

1. Exchange reserves in sterling held by central monetary institutions and international organisations.
2. The valuation of these public sector liabilities differs from that used for the official reserves. Total official debt outstanding at end-January 1994 valued on the same basis as the official reserves was $30 496 million.

Source: Bank of England, Quarterly Bulletin, and Central Statistical Office, Financial Statistics.

Table I. General government appropriation account

£ billion

	Taxes on income	Taxes on expenditure	Social security contributions	Property and entrepreneurial income[1]	Total current receipts	Final consumption	Subsidies	Debt interest	Current transfers[2]	Total current expenditure	Current surplus	Gross capital formation	Net capital transfers[3]	Net lending	Net lending per cent of GDP
1984	46.7	52.7	22.3	12.7	134.5	71.2	7.5	15.7	43.7	138.1	-3.6	7.0	-2.0	-12.6	-3.9
1985	51.6	56.7	24.2	14.6	147.1	75.3	7.2	17.6	48.8	148.9	-1.8	7.3	-0.9	-10.1	-2.8
1986	52.0	62.9	26.2	12.8	153.8	80.9	6.3	17.1	51.7	156.0	-2.2	7.3	0.2	-9.3	-2.4
1987	55.7	69.0	28.6	13.2	166.5	87.0	6.3	17.9	54.1	165.3	1.2	7.1	0.1	-5.8	-1.4
1988	61.7	76.0	32.1	13.6	183.5	93.6	6.0	18.2	55.4	173.3	10.2	6.2	0.6	4.6	1.0
1989	70.1	80.0	32.9	15.5	198.4	101.8	5.8	18.9	58.3	184.8	13.6	9.4	0.5	4.7	0.9
1990	76.7	78.3	34.7	23.4	213.1	112.9	6.1	18.7	63.5	201.2	11.8	12.8	-5.6	-6.6	-1.2
1991	74.9	84.8	36.4	22.3	218.4	124.2	6.0	17.0	70.2	217.4	1.0	12.3	-4.2	-15.5	-2.7
1992	73.5	87.6	37.3	21.9	220.2	132.7	6.8	17.1	84.4	240.9	-20.7	12.6	-4.5	-37.8	-6.4
1993	72.6	91.1	38.6	22.3	224.5	136.9	7.7	18.4	92.6	255.6	-31.1	11.3	-5.8	-48.3	-7.7
Seasonally adjusted															
1993 1	17.8	22.4	9.6	5.6	55.4	33.9	2.0	5.0	22.9	63.8	-8.3	3.7	-1.7	-13.7	-8.9
2	18.3	22.7	9.5	5.5	56.1	34.2	1.8	4.0	23.0	63.0	-6.9	2.9	-1.6	-11.4	-7.4
3	18.3	22.8	9.7	5.8	56.5	34.3	1.9	4.7	23.5	64.4	-7.9	2.8	-1.2	-11.8	-7.5
4	18.0	23.2	9.8	5.5	56.5	34.6	2.0	4.7	23.2	64.6	-8.0	2.0	-1.3	-11.3	-7.0

1. Includes community charge (from 2nd quarter of 1989) which is not treated as a tax on expenditure.
2. Social security, other grants to personal sector and net current grants paid abroad.
3. Taxes on capital and net grants and other transfers.
Source: Central Statistical Office, *Financial Statistics.*

Table J. Foreign trade by area
$ million, monthly averages

	1981	1982	1983	1984	1985	1986	1987	1988	1989	1990	1991	1992	1993 [1]
Imports, cif													
OECD	6 724	6 633	6 833	7 184	7 626	8 855	10 873	13 384	13 962	15 792	14 605	15 274	..
of which:													
North America	1 272	1 183	1 142	1 237	1 264	1 228	1 468	1 912	2 070	2 477	2 314	2 293	2 290
OECD Europe	4 946	4 912	5 135	5 406	5 780	6 890	8 502	10 331	10 745	12 089	11 113	11 685	..
of which:													
EC	3 844	3 905	4 034	4 200	4 503	5 468	6 784	8 303	8 691	9 776	9 025	9 585	..
Central and Eastern European countries	30	29	29	30	32	42	50	57	58	64	54	54	48
Developing countries	1 794	1 628	1 465	1 535	1 486	1 565	1 820	2 231	2 350	2 698	2 702	2 920	3 074
of which:													
OPEC	603	482	331	286	277	202	207	250	265	389	366	406	417
Total	8 548	8 290	8 327	8 750	9 144	10 463	12 743	15 673	16 370	18 553	17 361	18 248	..
Exports, fob													
OECD	6 104	5 853	5 729	6 021	6 643	6 921	8 569	9 516	10 055	12 386	12 457	12 663	..
of which:													
North America	1 204	1 220	1 182	1 271	1 438	1 482	1 770	1 872	1 956	2 219	1 929	2 039	2 174
OECD Europe	4 609	4 334	4 291	4 474	4 904	5 101	6 377	7 137	7 502	9 468	9 956	10 058	..
of which:													
EC	3 778	3 584	3 566	3 716	4 139	4 294	5 391	6 098	6 455	8 165	8 725	8 850	..
Central and Eastern European countries	73	56	49	50	53	61	71	84	83	104	98	89	91
Developing countries	2 420	2 173	1 859	1 766	1 751	1 882	2 166	2 364	2 454	2 760	2 736	2 905	3 060
of which:													
OPEC	932	850	666	561	555	578	625	641	693	725	748	776	712
Total	8 597	8 082	7 636	7 837	8 446	8 864	10 806	11 964	12 592	15 250	15 291	15 658	..

1. Due to a new statistical system measuring trade within the European Single Market, data for EC countries will be available later.
Source: OECD, *Foreign Trade Statistics.*

Table K. **Domestic finance**

	Change in wide monetary base* M0	Change in broad money M4	General government borrowing requirement	Sterling lending to private sector by banks	Net increase in building society shares and deposits	Building society new commitments to mortgages	Government securities-calculated redemption yields [1]			Local authority deposits, 3-months rates	Comparison between local authority and Euro-dollar, 3-month rates [2]
							Short-dated	Medium-dated	Long-dated		
	£ million						% per annum			% per annum at end of period	
1984	244	23 430	9 689	30 314	8 572	24 631	11.29	11.27	10.69	10.13	0.29
1985	182	25 873	8 398	34 024	7 462	27 763	11.13	11.06	10.62	11.94	0.08
1986	260	34 714	3 288	47 085	6 592	37 850	10.01	10.06	9.87	11.31	0.25
1987	209	42 481	-603	53 109	7 328	36 781	9.36	9.57	9.48	9.00	0.33
1988	401	52 509	-9 155	83 077	13 052	51 314	9.66	9.67	9.36	13.19	0.38
1989	336	64 393	-7 126	88 916	7 895	47 902	10.71	10.18	9.58	15.03	0.42
1990	158	51 635	-1 506	71 227	6 582	43 039	12.10	11.80	11.08	14.00	0.51
1991	185	30 003	8 354	36 787	6 006	41 862	10.18	10.11	9.92	10.93	0.08
1992	177	18 852	29 415	24 855	499	32 892	8.95	9.07	9.13	7.00	0.16
1993	376	27 607	44 362	22 448	2 143	33 853	6.65	7.47	7.87	5.31	0.12
1993 1	112	5 849	11 395	4 211	709	7 829	6.87	7.99	8.62	5.88	0.06
2	25	4 557	13 546	3 770	1 862	9 593	7.12	8.00	8.46	6.00	0.04
3	110	5 895	10 980	8 739	-135	8 476	6.55	7.22	7.51	5.94	-0.01
4	129	11 306	8 441	5 728	-293	7 955	6.06	6.67	6.87	5.31	0.12

* Seasonally adjusted.
1. Figures are the average of working days.
2. Difference between the local authority rate net of the cost of forward cover and the Euro-dollar rate, last working day figures.
Source: Bank of England, *Quarterly Bulletin*, and Central Statistical Office, *Financial Statistics*.

Table L. **Labour market indicators**
1979-1993

A. Evolution

	Peak		Trough		1989	1990	1991	1992	1993
					Per cent of total labour force				
Standardised unemployment rate	1983	12.4	1979	5.0	7.1	6.9	8.7	9.9	10.3
Unemployment rates									
Total	1986	11.6	1979	4.6	6.3	5.8	8.1	9.8	10.3
Male[1]	1993	14.0	1979	5.5	7.7	7.1	10.7	12.9	14.0
Female[1]	1986	8.9	1990	3.3	4.0	3.3	4.6	5.1	5.5
Youth (under 25 years)[1]	1983	23.4	1990	8.1	8.3	8.1	12.8	15.2	15.8
Share of long-term unemployment[2]	1985	48.6	1992	23.2	38.9	32.4	26.0	23.2	26.3
Vacancy rate	1988	8.8	1981	3.4	7.7	6.1	4.2	4.2	4.7

B. Structural or institutional characteristics

	1984	1989	1990	1991	1992	1993
			Per cent			
Participation rates[3,4]						
Global	77.6	80.1	80.3	79.8	78.9	78.5
Male	88.0	88.4	88.4	87.8	86.5	85.6
Female	66.1	71.1	71.5	71.2	70.6	70.8
Part-time employment rates[3,5]						
Global	19.3	20.2	20.3	20.8	22.1	22.8
Male	3.1	3.7	4.1	4.3	5.1	5.6
Female	43.0	42.4	41.9	42.5	43.7	44.2
Work-related government training programmes (thousand)[6]	194	457	423	363	339	324
Self-employment rate[7]	10.9	12.9	12.9	12.8	12.6	12.6

1. Per cent of respective labour force.
2. People looking for a job since one year or more as a percentage of total unemployment.
3. Data are the Spring non-seasonally adjusted data of the Labour Force Survey and are for Great Britain.
4. Defined as the total labour force divided by the population of working age (16-59/64).
5. Per cent of total employment of the relevant category.
6. Estimates of numbers consist of those participants in programmes and schemes(YTS, JTS, ET) who in the course of their participation in the programmes receive training in the context of a workplace but are not employees, self-employed or HM Forces.
7. Per cent of total employment.
Source: Department of Employment, *Employment Gazette;* OECD, *Labour Force Statistics.*

Table M. **Production structure and performance indicators**

	GDP share 1990 prices				Employment share (employees)			
	1982	1985	1990	1992	1982	1985	1990	1992
	Per cent							
A. Production structure								
Agriculture, forestry and fishing	2.1	2.1	1.9	2.1	1.7	1.6	1.3	1.3
Production industries:	26.7	27.7	29.8	28.3	30.7	31.0	31.9	31.6
Mining	3.4	3.3	2.2	2.3	1.7	1.4	0.8	0.6
Energy and water supply	2.3	2.3	2.3	2.3	2.3	2.3	2.3	2.3
Manufacturing (revised definition)	23.5	23.5	23.7	23.1	27.3	25.0	22.2	20.6
Construction	6.0	6.2	7.2	5.8	5.0	4.8	4.7	4.2
Services industries:								
Distribution, hotels and catering; repairs	13.0	13.6	14.2	13.9	19.3	20.0	21.2	21.4
Transport and communication	7.7	7.9	8.4	8.6	6.4	6.2	6.0	6.0
Banking, finance, insurance, business services and leasing	17.2	17.8	18.6	19.0	8.9	10.2	12.4	12.4
Other services [1]	24.7	23.5	21.6	22.8	28.1	29.4	30.3	32.2
Total	62.6	62.8	62.8	64.3	62.7	65.8	69.9	72.0

	1986	1987	1988	1989	1990	1991	1992	1993
B. Productivity growth [2]								
Whole economy	4.1	2.7	1.5	-0.3	-0.1	0.4	2.1	3.2
Total production industries	5.9	5.2	3.9	2.2	1.7	2.5	5.1	5.8
of which:								
Manufacturing (revised definition)	3.9	5.4	5.6	4.1	1.9	1.2	4.4	4.3

1. Including sewage and refuse disposal.
2. Output per person employed, based on the output measure of GDP. The employed labour force comprises employees in employment, the self-employed and HM Forces.
Source: Central Statistical Office, *Blue Book;* Department of Employment, *Employment Gazette.*

Table N. **Public sector**

	1980	1985	1990	1992	1993
	Per cent of GDP				
A. Structure of expenditure and taxation					
Expenditure, total	43.0	44.0	39.9	43.3	43.5
Current consumption	21.6	21.1	20.5	22.3	21.8
Transfers to households	11.3	13.7	11.5	14.2	14.8
Subsidies	2.5	2.0	1.1	1.1	1.2
Fixed investment	2.5	2.0	2.3	2.1	1.8
Other	5.1	5.2	4.4	3.6	3.9
Tax receipts, total	39.7	43.0	38.8	40.4	40.1
Income tax	13.4	14.4	13.9	12.3	11.6
of which:					
Personal income tax	11.1	10.6	11.2	10.9	10.2
Corporate profits tax	2.3	3.9	2.8	1.4	1.3
Social security contributions	10.6	12.7	10.7	13.4	14.0
Taxes on goods and services	15.7	15.9	14.2	14.7	14.5
Memorandum item:					
Net lending	−3.4	−2.8	−1.2	−6.4	−7.7

	1980	1985	1992
	Per cent		
B. Taxation			
Personal income tax			
Lowest marginal tax rate	30	30	20
Highest marginal tax rate	60	60	40
Number of brackets[1]	6	6	3
Marginal income tax rate			
(for single average production worker)	30	30	25
Social security contributions			
Marginal contribution rate			
(for single average production worker)	20.5	19.5	19.2
of which:			
Employees' contribution rate	6.75	9	9
Employers' contribution rate	13.75	10.5	10.2
Corporate income tax rate[2]	52	40	33
VAT standard rate[3]	15.0	15.0	17.5

1. There were two tax brackets until 31 March 1991.
2. The corporate income tax rate was 34 per cent until 31 March 1991.
3. VAT standard rate was 15 per cent until 31 March 1991.
Source: Central Statistical Office; OECD, *The Tax/Benefit Position of Production Workers;* International Bureau of Fiscal Documentation, *European taxation* (various issues).

Table O. **Financial markets**

	1980	1985	1990	1992
Size of financial sector				
Sector employment/total employment (all persons – per cent)	1.7	1.9	2.2	2.2[1]
Financial assets/GDP (Banks only)	1.0	1.7	1.9	1.9
Density of banking network[2]	..	24.0	22.6	..
Securities market capitalisation/GDP	1.2	3.1	3.8	3.5
Structure				
Share of intermediated financing in total financing	..	..	..	..
Financial institutions' share of financial assets	..	55.1	55.8	54.3
Household sector portfolio (share of total financial assets):				
Short-term assets	..	..	36.7	33.4
Long-term assets	..	..	63.3	66.6
Non-financial corporate sector portfolio:				
(share of total financial liabilities)				
Debt	53.4	51.0	51.6	..
Short-term	42.7	42.5	31.7	..
Long-term	10.7	8.5	19.9	..
Equity	46.6	49.0	48.4	..
Share capital	18.2	8.0	7.3	..
Retained earnings and other	28.4	41.0	41.1	..
Internationalisation of markets				
Foreign banking presence in domestic banking sector:[3]				
Assets	68.5	72.6	59.7	63.3
Liabilities	63.8	64.8	50.0	52.3
International banking networks:				
Number of foreign banks[4]	214	293	..	..
Branches of domestic banks abroad	..	..	..	..
Share of cross-border transactions:[5]				
Net purchases of foreign securities by domestic residents	29.9	164.1	–137.2	366.6[1]
Net purchases of domestic securities by foreign residents	12.9	94.7	–55.3	197.2[1]
Other indicators (all commercial banks – per cent)				
Interest rate margins[6]	3.77[7]	3.1	2.9	2.7
Operating expenses to total assets	3.44[7]	3.1	3.1	3.0

1. 1991.
2. Number of commercial bank branches/100 000 population.
3. As a percentage of commercial banks' balance sheets.
4. Number of branches and subsidiaries.
5. Ratio of cross-border portfolio transactions to net issues of securities on domestic securities market.
6. Interest income minus interest expenses divided by total assets.
7. Break in series in after 1984.
Source: Central Statistical Office, *Financial Statistics, Blue Book;* OECD, *Bank profitability.*

BASIC STATISTICS

BASIC STATISTICS:

INTERNATIONAL COMPARISONS

	Units	Reference period [1]	Australia	Austria
Population				
Total	Thousands	1991	17 292	7 823
Inhabitants per sq. km	Number	1991	2	93
Net average annual increase over previous 10 years	%	1991	1.5	0.3
Employment				
Total civilian employment (TCE) [2]	Thousands	1991	7 705	3 482
Of which: Agriculture	% of TCE		5.5	7.4
Industry	% of TCE		24.2	36.9
Services	% of TCE		70.4	55.8
Gross domestic product (GDP)				
At current prices and current exchange rates	Bill. US$	1991	297.4	164.7
Per capita	US$		17 200	21 048
At current prices using current PPP's [3]	Bill. US$	1991	280	135.6
Per capita	US$		16 195	17 329
Average annual volume growth over previous 5 years	%	1991	2.8	3.3
Gross fixed capital formation (GFCF)	% of GDP	1991	20.5	25.1
Of which: Machinery and equipment	% of GDP		8.8	10.4
Residential construction	% of GDP		4.6	4.6 (90
Average annual volume growth over previous 5 years	%	1991	0.3	5.2
Gross saving ratio [4]	% of GDP	1991	17.2	25.6
General government				
Current expenditure on goods and services	% of GDP	1991	18.3	18.2
Current disbursements [5]	% of GDP	1991	36.6	45.7
Current receipts	% of GDP	1991	33.7	47.2
Net official development assistance	% of GDP	1991	0.35	0.33
Indicators of living standards				
Private consumption per capita using current PPP's [3]	US$	1991	9 827	9 591
Passenger cars, per 1 000 inhabitants	Number	1990	430	382
Telephones, per 1 000 inhabitants	Number	1990	448 (89)	589
Television sets, per 1 000 inhabitants	Number	1989	484	475
Doctors, per 1 000 inhabitants	Number	1991	2	2.1
Infant mortality per 1 000 live births	Number	1991	7.1	7.4
Wages and prices (average annual increase over previous 5 years)				
Wages (earnings or rates according to availability)	%	1991	5.4	5.2
Consumer prices	%	1991	6.7	2.5
Foreign trade				
Exports of goods, fob*	Mill. US$	1991	39 764	40 985
As % of GDP	%		13.4	24.9
Average annual increase over previous 5 years	%		13.2	12.8
Imports of goods, cif*	Mill. US$	1991	38 844	48 914
As % of GDP	%		13.1	29.7
Average annual increase over previous 5 years	%		10.1	13.7
Total official reserves [6]	Mill. SDR's	1991	11 432	6 591
As ratio of average monthly imports of goods	Ratio		3.5	1.6

*   At current prices and exchange rates.
1. Unless otherwise stated.
2. According to the definitions used in OECD *Labour Force Statistics.*
3. PPP's = Purchasing Power Parities.
4. Gross saving = Gross national disposable income minus private and government consumption.
5. Current disbursements = Current expenditure on goods and services plus current transfers and payments of property income.
6. Gold included in reserves is valued at 35 SDR's per ounce. End of year.
7. Including Luxembourg.